Moll Dyer
and
OTHER WITCH TALES
OF SOUTHERN MARYLAND

Lynn J. Buonviri

THE
History
PRESS

Published by The History Press
Charleston, SC
www.historypress.com

Front cover illustration by Sarah Haynes.

First published 2019

Manufactured in the United States

ISBN 9781467141291

Library of Congress Control Number: 2019945082

Dedication

This book is dedicated to the memory of Mary Dyer, born on February 19, 1634, in Devon, England, and died in 1697 in St. Mary's County, Maryland. She was an incredibly strong and independent woman who lived her life taking care of her family and neighbors. To support herself in a period when common peasant women were invisible, she practiced herbal medicine and became the object of suspicion, ridicule and contempt as a result of conditions over which she had no control. She survived famine, disease and hardship and did not deserve to die at the hands of her neighbors. She should receive recognition of that fact and her influence in the community for over three hundred years.

Mary, known to all as Moll Dyer, has led me down the path all the way to write this book and taken the time to tap me on the shoulder from time to time to remind me that she was in control. I have also come to believe that she is a relieved and grateful old woman who has wanted to have her story told for centuries. Maybe in the telling of it I can bring some comfort and peace to her soul.

Moll Dyer's homestead. *Original illustration by artist Thomas Gallagher, St. Mary's College of Maryland.*

Contents

Acknowledgements

My special thanks to Susan Wolfe, Christina Dunbar, Linda Vert, Karen Wood, Frankie Tippett, Linda Reno and Peter Himmelheber of the St. Mary's County Historical Society, whose encouragement and assistance with research were essential to the success of this endeavor. Thomas Mattingly and Kennedy Abell from the Leonardtown Volunteer Fire Department made significant contributions to my research and understanding of the historical context for St. Mary's County families.

I owe a special debt of gratitude to my dear friends Bonnie Glod, Faye Snyder and Christine Trent. Without them, their help and their kind encouragement I would never have embarked on this adventure of enlightenment with the legendary witch Moll Dyer.

To my husband, Mike, thank you for being my first line editor and critic and for making me write and rewrite it until it was good. I so appreciate your belief in me and your patience and determination to have me be successful. You are my heart.

My sons David and Drew inspire me every day to make them proud of their mother. To my granddaughter Mickey and my grandson Reid, I hope that you will see that anything is possible if you set your mind to it, even if it is late in life. Andy and Ariadna, Katie, Nate and Maria, Carlo, Paolo and Matteo, I thank you all for your sweet encouragement and energy to complete this long endeavor.

I also would like to thank Tobacco Barn Distillery, St. Mary's County Genealogical Society, Major William Thomas Chapter of the National

Society of the Daughters of the American Revolution, Surratt House (Laurie Verge, Julie Cowdery and Susan Proctor), Samuel A. Mudd House and Museum and Mudd family members. They have all encouraged my endeavors by publishing my article and inviting me to talk about this incredible journey and the rewarding results. This has been a lovely trip with you all.

Walter Knowles, you have my eternal gratitude for being my mentor, friend and forever cheerleader. You have always encouraged me to dive into my projects head first and persevere until they were completed.

To Kate Jenkins at Arcadia Press, I owe you everything. You have been so patient and encouraging at every step of this process. There would not have been this book without your professional guidance, and I thank you completely.

Moll Dyer's Stone

In a corner of Leonardtown there stands a stone
Holding the spirit of a woman who died all alone.
Moll Dyer knew her herbs, she lived by herself
She had no need of others, their religion, their wealth.
In the year of our Lord, 1697,
There came a blizzard that rattled the heavens.
The winter was like nothing seen before.
"It's the work of that Witch!"
the townspeople swore.
They ran through the woods, torches afire.
Out to the shack of the Witch, known as
Moll Dyer.
Moll saw them coming, she slipped out the back.
To the ground the townspeople burned that old shack.
On that cold winter's night so long ago,
Moll ran for her life, through the woods in the snow.
The snow came down heavy, the wind lashed at her back!
The thunder roared, the lightning cracked!
On her knees she fell to that old stone.
Pursued, hated, cold, and alone.
Moll cursed the villagers and their seed for all time—
Impressed in the stone for the spell to bind.
Now, the people of Leonardtown give that stone a wide berth.
Fearing the woman, the legend, the curse.
Whether she was a Witch or just a lonely old soul,
The stone is still standing holding the spirit of Moll.

Foreword

In the fall of 2012, I agreed to undertake a very significant archival project for the Dr. Samuel A. Mudd House and Museum, located in Waldorf, Maryland. And yes, I am referring to the very same Dr. Samuel A. Mudd who, in 1865, was tried and convicted of complicity in the infamous assassination of the president of the United States, Abraham Lincoln.

On that particularly crisp fall morning six years ago, Danny Fluhart, the ever-dedicated and devoted president of the Dr. Samuel A. Mudd House and Museum, approached me and apprised me of the voluminous, though unorganized and unpreserved, collection of primary and secondary documents, newspaper and magazine accounts and other Lincoln assassination–related material—specifically chronicling the alleged involvement of Dr. Mudd in the conspiracy to murder President Lincoln—extant in the museum's Exhibit Hall. Additionally, there existed a veritable trove of primary documents, newspaper accounts and sundry Mudd family memoirs, all of which, in sum, chronicled the founding, developmental growth and successful preservation of the Dr. Samuel A. Mudd House and Museum.

As a trained historian, and one who has had a lifelong fascination with the Lincoln assassination machinations, I jumped at the opportunity to apply the essentials of the historian's craft in both preserving and archiving these most significant and historically valuable materials. The initial enthusiasm I felt when laying out the scope of this project was soon blunted by the daunting realization that I desperately needed competent help to assist in the identification, organization and compilation of the materials at hand. It was then that I had the great, good fortune to meet Lynn Buonviri, a docent at the Mudd House Museum, who had graciously volunteered her talents in assisting me in this worthy project.

Upon our introduction, Lynn, a thirty-year denizen of Southern Maryland and an active volunteer participant in both local and regional historical and cultural organizations, elicited that she had scant experience in archival or preservation activities but did, however, possess a sincere interest in bringing her talents to bear in assisting in the development and implementation of the Mudd House Museum historical resource-preservation project. I was immediately impressed by Lynn's direct style of communication and her willingness to take on something clearly new and challenging, solely because of her interest in regional historical interpretation.

As autumn's brilliance faded into the slate-gray skies of winter, Lynn and I logged hours upon hours laboring away the passing time, sorting through binders of material, evaluating the significance of each document and developing a schematic outline for organizing the thousands of pages that lay before us. Lynn's obvious organizational and analytical skills, reflections of her many years' experience as an educator and Information Technology professional, proved invaluable in completing the archival project. Indeed, Lynn brought her talent to the forefront when she, with very little assistance from me other than nodding encouragement, produced a computerized, searchable database containing over ten thousand reference items. I was stunned by the breadth and detail that was her automated opus and simultaneously amazed at the sheer determination she applied in constructing this historian's and researcher's dream come true!

Aside from the marvelous friendship we cultivated over those many months constructing the Mudd archive and preserving its contents into a fifty-four-set archival collection, it was I who most benefitted from my collaboration with Ms. Buonviri. Her knowledge, inquisitiveness and enthusiasm regarding regional Southern Maryland history and culture are both impressive and fascinating.

Her varied interests in local history and lore have led her to pursuing highly detailed and determined research culminating in print publications regarding historically obscure individuals, such as Private Jane Perkins, a female Civil War soldier from Virginia who did not disguise her gender identity, fought for the Confederacy, was captured by Union forces and confined in the Federal prisoner-of-war camp at Point Lookout, Maryland, where she reputedly gave birth to an infant while incarcerated therein, to instantly recognizable persons, like Mary Surratt, whose unfortunate association with John Wilkes Booth and his fellow conspirators led to her still controversial and decidedly untimely death by execution at the end of a rope in 1865. In each of these pursuits, Lynn utilized determined and exhaustive research methodologies necessary to bring credibility and factuality to the interesting subject matter at hand.

And now, Ms. Buonviri has graced you and me with yet another very fine publication, the subject of which (pun intended) is the legendary witch of Southern Maryland, Moll Dyer. Poor Moll Dyer, the unfortunate and reclusive old woman who was alleged to have possessed the powers of the ancients, was subsequently hounded away from her home in the depths of a harsh winter's night by a superstitious mob, which, the following morning, discovered her frozen, lifeless body lying perched upon a substantially sized rock. Moll receives sympathetic yet thorough treatment from the author. Local lore, and indeed, strange and eerie occurrences attributed to the personage of Moll Dyer, come to life and are presented and explored by Ms. Buonviri in a highly intriguing and entertaining fashion, thus guaranteeing satisfaction from even the most casual of readers.

What I find most intriguing about Lynn's latest offering is her superb genealogical analysis of Moll Dyer's ancestry. By way of her usual dogged and determined research style and acumen, Ms. Buonviri has successfully unraveled the mystery of who the real Moll Dyer was, whence she came and when. In due fashion, Lynn credibly identifies many of Moll Dyer's real-life Southern Maryland relatives, some of whom will surely surprise you!

As evident within the pages of *Moll Dyer and Other Witch Tales of Southern Maryland*, Ms. Buonviri has once again mined wonderfully fascinating and factual material that she has woven into yet another interesting and curious chapter of the story that is Southern Maryland. Along with her incisive and entertaining treatment of Private Jane Perkins, CSA, Mrs. Mary Surratt and now Moll Dyer, as they say in show business, "The hits just keep on comin'!"

—Walter Knowles
Burke, Virginia

How This Project Began

I began my journey to find the true identity of Moll Dyer in 2013. Why did I dedicate that much time to this effort? It all started for two reasons.

First, as a resident of St. Mary's County, Maryland, since 1981, I have found it impossible to ignore the legend of Moll Dyer. The story of her fate and the curse of the rock have always fascinated me. I have resided about one mile from Moll Dyer Run and Moll Dyer Road since 1986 and roamed the woods in that area extensively with my bloodhounds. My curiosity was primed thinking of this unusual neighbor and her dramatic saga.

Second, my life since 2005 has involved giving tours as a docent at Surratt House and Tavern in Clinton, Maryland, and at the Dr. Samuel A. Mudd House and Museum in Waldorf, Maryland. In telling the story of Dr. Mudd, one of the facts of his life is that his wife was named Sarah Frances Dyer. I was instantly curious about the connection between the Dyer name for Sarah Frances and the Moll Dyer legend. I volunteered to be involved with historian Walter Knowles in a project in 2012–13 to catalogue a large number of family articles, documents and photographs for the Mudd House Library. This included cataloguing and indexing fifty-four loose-leaf notebooks containing hundreds of Mudd family documents, including the letters containing the efforts to exonerate Dr. Mudd and restore his name and reputation. Reading the documents was necessary to determine the categories to identify the contents.

Dr. Richard Dyer Mudd was Dr. Samuel Mudd's grandson and spent his entire life campaigning to multiple presidents to exonerate his grandfather.

He sought to clear the family name since the 1865 conviction of Dr. Mudd for complicity in the assassination of Abraham Lincoln. Knowing that the efforts of his entire life resulted in no change for his grandfather's status gave me an appreciation of the intense desire of the Mudd family to restore its reputation. Delving into these records piqued my interest to find out whether or not Sarah Frances Dyer Mudd was related to the witch of St. Mary's County, Moll Dyer. Would having a witch in the family tree add to the intrigue of the Mudd family saga and reputation? How would the family members react to having another infamous ancestor? Those questions drove me to begin the search for answers.

The quest for answers started with a visit to the St. Mary's County Historical Society to retrieve all the genealogical facts pertaining to Moll Dyer. My inquiry was met with the discovery that nothing of fact was known about Moll Dyer, including whether or not she even existed. From then, the gauntlet was thrown down for me, and I took on the challenge.

I looked for any factual information that I could find to identify the woman who *could* be Moll Dyer. I emphasize the word *could*. This has never been an ironclad proof of who she was but rather the search for a woman who fit all the known facts and survived any onslaughts from any contradicting challenges. The thought of challenges to the results is putting the cart before the horse; the focus was on the search to find out who she was. First, I set out to examine those who claimed to be related to her and to trace each of their roots back to ancestors in the early to mid-seventeenth century. Developing those family trees took several months. See the appendix for the complete details of that genealogical research. There were five individuals to research. When their lineages were complete, there appeared one woman who fit. Five years later, this work has emerged. I hope that you enjoy the vast research that went into documenting the life of Moll Dyer.

Part One

BACKGROUND

1

The Legend of Moll Dyer

Who was Moll Dyer? Was she a witch? These are two questions that inspired the journey to find out the answers. First, here is the legend that started that journey.

The legend of Moll Dyer is a story of witchcraft and what happened to an alleged witch in St. Mary's County, Maryland, in 1697. According to the legend, Moll was an elderly single woman who resided in a hut in the area just south of the county seat, Leonardtown, around a road now called Moll Dyer Road. At the time, the town did not exist. She was an elderly spinster who practiced some strange customs that were foreign to the other residents of the county. Since this was the 1690s, her unusual habits caused the local residents to think of her and label her as a witch. When disastrous events occurred in the area, like disease outbreaks and crop failures, she became the logical object of blame.

In the record cold winter of 1697, disease (probably influenza) broke out in the area, and many became sick and died. The focus of blame for it was Moll Dyer. As the winter progressed, conditions steadily became more and more severe, and the number of citizen deaths increased. The people were afraid of the witch and hesitated to incur her wrath by telling her that they wanted her to leave the area. To avoid her but get rid of her, they decided to force her to leave the area.

In a desperate act to force her out, a group of local townspeople descended on her hut in the dead of an extremely cold winter night and set her house on fire. She fled the fire and ran into the nearby woods, and the citizens

Moll Dyer on rock. *Sketch by author Nicole Canfield.*

thought that they were rid of her. A few days later, however, she was found frozen to death on a large rock by a young man out searching for some stray farm animals in the dense woods. When her frozen body was removed from the rock, her hand and knee prints had made indentations into the surface of the rock, and one arm was outstretched toward the heavens. The local folks attributed to the rock a curse that Moll had left in her dying moments for the people who had persecuted her and caused her death.[1]

Thus began over 320 years of a story that was passed down from generation to generation in St. Mary's County, Maryland. It was part of the legend that Moll had lived in the area where Moll Dyer Road is located near the stream referred to as Moll Dyer Run. Over the years, residents told of the cursed rock located in the thick woods on the property of those residents. How does such a story survive for so long without any basis in fact? There has to be some motivation to repeat the story through so many generations. Could there be an overriding sense of guilt by those who perpetuated the tragedy?

Eventually, the St. Mary's County Historical Society became interested in the rock as part of the legend and story that had been written about for years and initiated an effort to find and remove the infamous rock from the property where it was reportedly located. Their efforts were rewarded with the help of members and the cooperation of local citizens. Because one of the members of the historical society was a member of the National Guard, that organization also became involved in the effort.

In 1968, Philip Love went into the woods with the owner of the property, found the rock and documented his journey in an article for the *Washington Star*. There have been many articles written about Moll Dyer and her rock. However, it would remain in the woods until October 14, 1972. The local National Guard removed the 875-pound boulder from the woods and relocated it in Leonardtown next to the Old Jail, which is a historic landmark and now the St. Mary's County Visitors' Center.[2] On the surface of the rock, there are faint indentations where the hands and knees of Moll Dyer were frozen into it for all eternity.

During the location and removal process, those involved reported many incidents and accidents, which fueled the story of the curse left on this fieldstone by the irate Moll Dyer as she died. Philip Love reported injuries such as knee sprains and incidents when cameras failed to operate and glasses were broken. These events added to the growing legend of a curse before the rock arrived at its new location.

There are many local residents who described strange and unexplainable incidents in the Moll Dyer Road and Run area, and several of the accidents and incidents that occurred when the rock was removed were reported in the news articles written at the time. Personal injuries and automobile accidents as well as unusual weather events have been reported in the area. Many of these accounts were documented in an episode of the Weather Channel's *Supernatural* series, "The Legend of Moll Dyer." Karen Stauffer recalled an incident in autumn of 1980 when she went into the woods with two friends.

Moll Dyer Run. *Photo by the author.*

Moll Dyer Rock next to Old Jail, Leonardtown, Maryland. *Photo by the author.*

Old Jail Visitors' Center, Leonardtown, Maryland (1858). *Photo by the author.*

The weather conditions were calm and sunny, but as they walked through the Moll Dyer Run area, the weather worsened with high wind and thunder and lightning. They fled the woods, afraid of what had occurred to them in just that area. Residents of the Moll Dyer Road area have also reported automobile accidents with strange causes such as sighting apparitions that disappear after the accident. Other residents have suffered family tragedies over many years and attribute an unusually high number of these events to the fact that they descend from the citizens who burned the hut of Moll Dyer in 1697. The belief in the curse of Moll Dyer seems to be reinforced by incidents that actually occur or by a sort of mass guilt felt by the residents of that piece of woods, which causes them to attribute any unfortunate events to the legendary curse.

2
history of Witchcraft in Maryland[3]

It is important to understand the social climate in Maryland in the late seventeenth century to better appreciate the circumstances that controlled the fate of Moll Dyer. There had been trials of other accused witches in the Southern Maryland area that were held between 1650 and 1697, the period immediately preceding the events surrounding Moll's death.

Witchcraft was a felony in Maryland in the seventeenth century. Definitions of witchcraft were based on a book titled *Country Justice*, written by Michael Dalton. Published in England in the early part of the century, this book was a guide to English law for the use of justices of the peace and other officials. It was also used as a guide in Maryland for prosecution of cases of witchcraft. The 1690 edition of this book can be found in the Maryland Archives. For a conviction of felony witchcraft, testimony of two witnesses was required or a confession by the offending witch. However, because the offending acts were usually committed clandestinely, circumstantial evidence could be considered if strong enough.

Dalton made recommendations for criteria to be considered when officials were deciding whether or not to pursue an investigation for a witchcraft prosecution. The following list are these recommendations:

1. Witch has a familiar or spirit, which could appear as a man, woman, boy, dog, cat, foal, hare, rat, toad and so forth, and would have been named and christened.

2. The familiar would have a big or little teat on its body in a secret place, where the witch would suckle. He also leaves a mark on the witch's

body, maybe red or blue spot, that is sunken or hollow, may disappear and reappear, does not bleed if pricked and is located in a "secret part."

The Witchcraft Act of 1604 declared that making a pact with the devil was punishable by death, even if no harm was caused. Proving numbers 1 and 2 was sufficient to prove this, but anyone with a tick bite was susceptible to being convicted. Dalton went on to recommend the following thirteen criteria as evidence to also consider:

3. Possession of pictures/images of clay or wax, found in the home or roasted or buried in the earth would indicate who had been bewitched;

4. Cursing, bitter imprecations, threats were used for revenge;

5. The witch confessed his/her power to hurt, such as threats to do so (power of words was very significant at that time);

6. The witch inquires diligently about a sick party;

7. The witch appears as an apparition to the sick party in his fits;

8. The sick party (bewitched), in his fits, names the party suspected;

9. Neighbors report that suspected witch is kin, servant or familiar with a convicted witch;

10. Other witches confess their own witchcraft and testify against the suspected witch. (Since these were in league with the devil, their testimony alone was worthless, as they were considered liars. As today, testimony of a co-conspirator alone is not enough to convict an accused.);

11. Dead body bleeds when a suspected witch touches it;

12. Testimony of person hurt, upon his death;

13. Children or servants of suspected witch confess to circumstances listed in numbers 1–6;

14. Suspected witch voluntarily confesses to the hurt done and giving his or her soul to the devil. (Other evidence was required to corroborate the confession.);

15. Suspected witch possesses pictures of clay or wax, cut hair, bones, powders, books of witchcraft, charms and pots or places where spirits may be kept. (The place would stink!)

Dalton then wrote the evidences to prove that someone had been bewitched:

1. Healthy body suddenly taken (dies) without reason or natural cause;

2. Two or more taken (die) in strange fits in many things;

3. Afflicted party, in his fits, tells what the witch, or other absent parties, are doing or saying;

4. Parties do or say strange things and don't remember it;

5. Supernatural strength is exhibited, such as two strong men could not control a child or other weaker person;

6. Party vomits crooked pins, needles, nails, coals, lead, straw, hair;

7. Party sees visible apparition, and shortly after some mischief befalls him.

English and American authorities were not insane and knew natural events, as well as witches, could cause harm. They agreed to not jump to conclusions that witchcraft was to blame. There were many "medicine women" in this period who did good things for their communities. It was the allegiance expressed with the devil that crossed the line to black magic and felony witchcraft. This allegiance to the devil was outside the definition of religious belief. Once God was not a part of the belief system, the practice was not considered religious. Hence, it was not a part of religious tolerance because it was not then religious in nature.

Woman "bewitched" into spitting out crooked pins. *Original illustration by artist Ruby Bassford, St. Mary's College of Maryland.*

Witch with a toad, her "familiar." *Original illustration by artist Ruby Bassford, St. Mary's College of Maryland.*

Father Andrew White, a Jesuit priest who traveled to Maryland with the original settlers, firmly believed in the existence of witches and witchcraft. He attributed to witchcraft many of the unfortunate events and inclement weather encountered on the journey to Maryland. After his arrival in the colony, Father White blamed witches for any problems that arose, either among the settlers or among the tribes of Native Americans who were living all around their settlements. There was no doubt about his beliefs in his writing and journals.

Witch Bottles

Stories of witches and witchcraft have been told throughout recorded history. They survive today. Whether it was a crime or not for someone to practice witchcraft, the belief that witches existed has been a subject of discussion and possibility in society. People believed they needed to find ways to deal with or deter the threat of the presence of witchcraft and witches in their midst. There has been little, however, written or told about what could be done to counteract or deter a spell or curse by a witch. Evidently, the witch bottle has been one way known to do that for many centuries.

Witch bottles date as far back as the early 1500s and originated in Germany. The concept, if not the actual bottles, is believed to have traveled with English immigrants to America. Of course, they were immensely popular during the witch hysteria in Europe and America during the late seventeenth and early eighteenth centuries.

What exactly is a witch bottle? It is a bottle that is either glass or ceramic and holds approximately twelve to sixteen ounces. It will hold items that were used to stop a curse or turn the curse back to the witch. There are different recipes, but all of the items were for protecting the owner and stopping any perceived or detected curse. The array of items in the bottle were for specific purposes and aimed at the witch who was causing the problem. Items included pins, needles, nails, herbs, hair, urine or sulphur. To have all these in the brew would be preferred. This concoction would be boiled and placed in the bottle and then in a fire, hearth or the ground to work its magic. Boiling was key to the success of the potion. Sulphur, if available, was also thought to have special properties because it came from the "underworld" of the volcanoes. If the process was followed correctly, it would protect the victim and reverse the curse against the casting witch with the ultimate goal of killing him or her.

There are multiple options for the contents of a witch bottle. Some include wine and rosemary for the bottles to stop a curse, and others recommend that the bottle be buried in the farthest corner of the preparer's property. Another version of the witch bottle involved ingredients to invite good fortune instead of preventing or reversing bad fortune. For good fortune, or a love spell, the ingredients would include pleasant elements such as dried or crushed flower petals, rosemary and lavender and rosewater instead of urine. The bottle would then be sealed with red or pink wax and placed in a location where it would not be seen or disturbed.

The *Astrological Practice of Physick* (1671), by astrologist Joseph Blagrave, sums up the ancient belief about witch bottles this way:

> *Another way is to stop the urine of the Patient, close up in a bottle, and put into it three nails, pins, or needles, with a little white salt, keeping the urine always warm: if you let it remain long in the bottle, it will endanger the witches life; for I have found by experience that they will be greviously tormented making their water with great difficulty, if any at all....The reason...is because there is a part of the vital spirit of the Witch in it, for such is the subtlety of the Devil, that he will not suffer the Witch to infuse any poysonous matter into the body of a man or beast, without some of the Witches blood mingled with.*

The ingredients of the witch bottle had specific purposes. The nails, pins and/or needles were to impale the demon witch. The urine was to drown the witch. One specific example appears in a book about witchcraft by Joseph Glanvill from 1681.[4] The author reported that the process was followed and the bottle placed in the hearth to end a wife's affliction from a curse. When the bottle was placed in the fire, it exploded, supposedly because the witch had resisted the counter spell. The wife's affliction continued until a new witch bottle was prepared and buried upside down in the ground outside the entrance to the home. Once that was done, the curse was stopped. The wife recovered, and the supposed witch died.

These accounts illustrate the pervasive belief in witchcraft throughout history that can still be unearthed today. One such witch bottle discovery was made in Dorchester County, Maryland, in January 1983 at the site of a possible tenant house or slave quarter called the White Oak site.[5] A broken wine bottle was excavated around the location of the hearth or chimney.

Left: Single witch bottle replica. *Photo by the author.*

Below: Bartmann witch bottles (also known as greybeards and bellarmines) were made of salt-glazed stoneware, decorated with a stylized bearded (frequently malevolent) face mask. Origin Rhineland early sixteenth century. *Copyright Hampshire County Council. Provided by Hampshire Cultural Trust.*

While wine bottles are frequently found in archaeological excavations, and a broken one would not be remarkable, this one was different. The bottle contained the original solid stopper, imbedded with nickel-plated copper straight pins. These pins indicated that the scientists had unearthed a witch bottle. Since the bottle was broken, the other ingredients had long since been absorbed into the soil. The broken bottle was found in the same general area with bone and a horseshoe, which could have been associated with the ritual burial of the witch bottle. Iron, the horseshoe, is reported to hold its own protective powers. Archaeologists have unearthed other bottles at other sites in the general area and from the same period.

There are groups that still believe in the magic of these bottles and provide the recipes and instructions about making them on the internet. In addition, there are people who still believe and practice witchcraft, and they are all around. There are three women who claim to practice witchcraft today in St. Mary's County. Their beliefs are centered on growing herbs to use for home remedies, but they use the handbooks of witchcraft in their practices. Wonder what they would have to say about witch bottles?

Maryland officials prosecuted very few witchcraft cases because the state was founded on the principle of religious tolerance. This allowed the pursuit of many religions and stopped the religious persecution associated with the witchcraft hysteria that occurred in Salem, Massachusetts. That series of events was largely the result of religious prejudice toward the Catholics by the Puritans. Usually, the suspicion and accusations were aimed toward single women, whether never married or widowed. It seems that married women just never wanted to trust other single women.

Maryland Witch Trials

MARY LEE

Sailors are notoriously superstitious. They were in the 1600s and are still known to be so today, although knowledge of weather and other natural phenomena is much more advanced today. They were prone to blame any misfortune on supernatural forces, and witches were convenient targets for their wrath. Luck played a huge role when ships set out on journeys that lasted for months. It was considered lucky to start the journey on a Sunday, to have women and children onboard and to have cats with them. On the other hand, dogs, clergy and lawyers were considered unlucky to have aboard ship. Many voyages set out for the New World and were never heard from again, so it is understandable that the crew of the ships wanted to have as much luck on their side as possible.

The case of Mary Lee was the very first case of witchcraft for the colony of Maryland and happened before she arrived in the settlement. She was a passenger on the ship *Charity of London*, captained by John Bosworth. Having a witch on board was certainly very unlucky, especially with the connection of witches to the weather. Approximately three weeks before the ship arrived in Maryland, a rumor of the presence of a witch on the ship became a problem for the crew and passengers.

Apparently, she did not deny being a witch when confronted with the accusation, so the crew approached the captain and requested that a trial be held to take care of the problem. In order to avoid the situation, the captain said that he would put Mary ashore on one of the islands near Bermuda. That seemed satisfactory, but the prevailing winds prevented the ship from that destination. As the ship journeyed on, the problems continued and the crew pushed the captain to hold a trial. The captain delayed that action because of the complications associated with the legal requirements on the ship to hold a trial.

As the weather intervened and the sailors were left to their own devices, they searched Mary's body and supposedly found the mark of a witch. The next morning, the mark had disappeared, further adding to the evidence of witchcraft. She did not deny the accusation and did, in fact, confess to being a witch. When the crew again pressed the captain to hold a trial and put her to death, he refused to be a part of the process and told the crew to do what they felt they had to but to be in complete agreement to whatever outcome they decided. He retired to his quarters and wanted to know nothing about what they did. She was subsequently hanged and disposed of overboard.

The captain swore before the governor of Maryland on June 23, 1654, that the execution of Mary Lee had not been of his hand and that he had known nothing about the plans of the crew to carry it out. A Jesuit priest, who was on the *Charity* when this incident happened, filed a deposition stating his outrage at the proceedings. However, as his presence was considered unlucky, his opinion or attempt at intervention would not have been considered. There were others onboard who knew that what was happening was wrong but felt that they were powerless to stop the actions of the frenzied mob. Court officials recorded depositions from witnesses aboard the ship named Francis Darby and Henry Corbyn, a gentleman and a merchant, respectively, that corroborated the facts that had been described. No witness expressed any doubt that Mary had been a witch. There is also no record of anyone being prosecuted in the colony for any actions taken in this matter. Apparently, the authorities were satisfied to have the crew members take care of the problem on their own, extrajudicially, or outside the judicial process.

Elizabeth Richardson

Elizabeth Richardson was the second woman executed for being an alleged witch aboard a ship on the voyage to Maryland from England. This case was reported when John Washington, the great-grandfather of George

Washington, filed a complaint in 1659 against Edward Prescott, the owner of a ship named the *Sarah Artch*, who was present when the hanging was carried out. Being a capital offense, it was heard in the provincial court at St. Mary's City. John Washington was from Westmoreland County, Virginia, and returned to his home after filing the felony complaint.

Prescott was summarily arrested and charged with the murder of Elizabeth by the proprietary governor, Josias Fendall. Fendall then notified Washington that he would be expected to appear at the trial and confront Prescott with his accusation. The trial date was set for October 4 or 5. Fendall was very concerned with protection of the legal rights of the accused witch as well as the accused murderer and did his very best to carry out the right of the accused to be confronted in person by his accuser.

When Washington received the notice to appear at the trial, he wrote back to Fendall that he could not be there on the date set for the trial because of the baptism of his young son that was due to take place. Washington went on to tell Fendall that if Prescott could be bound over until the date of the next provincial court, he, as accuser, would try to be present. This letter was dated

Maryland Dove (replica). Travelers to Maryland in 1600s came in similar ships, and two witches were hanged en route. *Photo by Peg and Jim Healy.*

September 30, 1659. It seems that it was nearly impossible for Washington to make the trip back to St. Mary's City with such short notice, especially with the baptism already planned and guests invited from out of town.

When the defendant demanded a speedy trial, another right to which he was entitled, the trial went forth without Washington's presence. Prescott testified that he was indeed the owner of the ship and was present when the execution was carried out. He said that he had appointed a voyage master named John Greene for the trip. Prescott protested to Greene about the proceedings in which Elizabeth Richardson was accused of being a witch and the designated penalty of hanging. When he did, Greene and the crew threatened mutiny unless the sentence was carried out. Prescott presented the ship's documents filed with the harbormaster as evidence, and they corroborated his testimony. When Washington failed to appear to testify against him or dispute any of his claims, he asked that the judge find him not guilty of the felony accusation.

Although the law did not allow extrajudicial execution of witches, which would have been the case here and in the case of Mary Lee, Fendall and the court were forced to acquit the ship owner in this case because the one witness against Prescott did not appear. There is no record of anyone else being brought to trial for the killing of Elizabeth Richardson.

Elizabeth Bennett

On October 11, 1665, Elizabeth Bennett was accused of witchcraft, but General William Calvert refused to prosecute the case and she was cleared. The case was brought before the grand jury with charges "concerning witchcraft, Burglary, felony, murther [archaic spelling of murder] & other Trespasses," but no indictment was returned. She was cleared by unanimous proclamation of the grand jury. Nothing else about her is mentioned in the court records, and very little about her can be found anywhere else.

Upon further investigation of the Lois Green Carr Career Files, there is mention of one Richard Bennett, who was deceased by 1697. The following facts were revealed and may explain something about Elizabeth Bennett and why she might have been accused of being a witch.

Richard and Elizabeth Bennett are recorded as arriving in Maryland in 1646 with their four children. They had two sons, Thomas and Richard, and two daughters, Sarah and Mary. Richard is listed as having been born in 1614. Elizabeth may have been about the same age for them to have been married long enough to have four children in 1646.[6]

Shortly after their arrival, on July 15, 1647, there is a record of a legal deposition by Richard in which he testified against a man by the name of James Johnson and stated that Johnson had uttered treasonous dialogue against the governor of Maryland. He went on to ask that Johnson be incarcerated immediately because Richard was afraid for his life. There were multiple men named James Johnson in St. Mary's County at that time. One stands out, though: a James Johnson owned three parcels in Poplar Hill Hundred totaling six hundred acres. These were close to Richard Bennett's land. He was most likely a pretty powerful man in the area who had connections and influence with the Bennetts' neighbors.[7]

This same James Johnson appears in a record dated February 18, 1648–49, in which he gave a cow to Thomas Bennett, Richard's son, and it mentions Richard and Elizabeth in the transfer of this cow. Thomas had become a beneficiary of James's by this time, yet his father, Richard, was still alive. Could this indicate that the problem with the testimony given by Richard in the previous year had been resolved?[8]

St. Mary's City State House (replica), where witch trials were held. *Photo by the author.*

By July 16, 1651, an entry in the legal records shows that Elizabeth had buried Richard and married John Taylor, an "Ordinary Keeper." In this transaction of tobacco goods and livestock by son Richard, Elizabeth (Sarah), his mother, and John Taylor, her husband, were still recorded as residing in Poplar Hill on the Bennett land, the large portion of which had been passed down to the two sons, Thomas and Richard. Listed as witnesses to this action were James Johnson and Edward Williams. James Johnson would appear to be a friend and neighbor for the Bennett family from his constant presence in their legal actions.[9]

Just four years later, Elizabeth is listed as the wife of William Wilkes and the widow of John Taylor on the record dated August 16, 1655.[10] At this point, she had three husbands in four years, but that is not the end of the story. By the end of 1655, she was again listed as widow Elizabeth Wilkes, after burying three husbands in four years.[11] Could this series of dead husbands be part of the charge of witchcraft that was filed against her in 1665? The word *murther* in the charging document might be a clue about that, but maybe her friend James Johnson, an influential citizen and neighbor, had some connections that would have worked in her favor. Maybe, too, she married again and evaded the curse of being a widow or spinster—in other words, a single woman. At any rate, nothing further about her life has of yet been discovered.

JOHN COWMAN

The case of John Cowman is interesting because he is the only man brought to trial for practicing witchcraft in the state. Until that time no one, man or woman, had been judicially prosecuted or successfully executed in Maryland. In 1674, John Cowman was charged with using witchcraft, sorcery or enchantment upon the body of Elizabeth Doodale as specified by the statute of King James of England. There are no accounts of the indictment or court proceedings, but the verdict was guilty of the charges and sentence was death by hanging. That is the beginning of the most puzzling part of this story.

John Cowman petitioned the Lower House of the General Assembly to intercede on his behalf for clemency and reprieve. No reasons or mitigating circumstances were given, but the Lower House did petition Charles Calvert, the lieutenant general and chief judge of the provincial court, for clemency.

The petition asked that the law be remitted and relaxed and that mercy be exercised on "so wretched and Miserable an Object." This was signed by Robert Ridgely, Upper House, February 17, 1674. The reason for this action is not known, but it certainly benefitted John Cowman's situation.

The lieutenant general considered the petition and agreed to stay the execution. Both Houses of the Assembly agreed on the condition that the sheriff of St. Mary's County carry out a mock hanging in which John would be put on the gallows with a rope around his neck. At that time, he was to acknowledge his debt to the Lower House of the Assembly for his life. From then on, he was to remain at St. Mary's City and be employed in services to be determined by the governor and council for whatever time period they saw fit. No doubt he relished being alive to be able to work at any task that would be specified by the governor and council.

The unique circumstances of this case make it extremely interesting. Not only was John Cowman the first and only man to be convicted and sentenced to death for witchcraft in Maryland, but he also was the only man to be charged. Then, to have the hanging stayed illustrated the more powerful role played by men in this period and how they were less likely to have to endure the consequences of being convicted of witchcraft.

St. Mary's City Farthing's Ordinary (replica), a business where John Cowman might have been put to work. *Photo by the author.*

REBECCA FOWLER

The most significant witch trial to occur in Maryland was that of Rebecca Fowler in 1685. On September 30, 1685, Rebecca Fowler was transferred to St. Mary's County sheriff's custody by the Calvert County sheriff. She was held pending the consideration of the grand jury, which was convened between September 29, 1685, and October 12 of the same year. The justices were listed as Thomas Tailler, Henry Darnall, William Digges, William Stevens and Nicholas Sewall. The members of the grand jury were Randolph Hinson, Richard Kenne, Hugh Hopewell Jr., John Atkey, Thomas Ford, Robert Cole, William Ferguson, Samuel Wheeler, John Kirke, Walter Lane, William Blankenstein, Joseph Spernon, Richard Holland, John Hinton, William Harris and William Morris.

In the charging document, Rebecca is referred to as the wife of planter John Fowler, but later in the same document she is called a spinster. The terms *wife* and *spinster* would indicate that she was the widow of planter John Fowler. The same document goes on to state that on August 31, 1685, at Mount Calvert Hundred, she was accused of using witchcraft on Francis Sandsbury (or Sansbury) and others to create illness, lameness and other maladies. The grand jury went on to return an indictment on the charges of "witchcraft, charmes, and sorceries," to which she pleaded not guilty.

A model courtroom in the statehouse where witch trials were held. *Photo by the author.*

A replica stockade outside of the statehouse, where witches were put on display for citizens to see. *Photo by the author.*

The case went to trial on October 2, 1685, before Attorney General Thomas Burford. The jurors were Randolph Brandt, Charles Egerton, James Yore, Michael Miller, Matthew Lewis, Edward Turner, John Taunt, Andrew Insley, Justinian Tennison, James Neale, Andrew Abbington and Abraham Rhoades. There is no record of the testimony given at the trial, but the results were that on October 3, 1685, Rebecca Fowler was found guilty and sentenced to hang by the neck until dead on October 9, 1685. The sentence was duly carried out. Rebecca Fowler was the first known person executed by Maryland government authorities for witchcraft.

That would be the end of the story except for the research done by Rebecca Logan for her doctoral dissertation, "Witches and Poisoners in Colonial Chesapeake," published in 2001, in which she uncovered facts to put together the personal story of Rebecca Fowler and others. Logan speculated in her work that Rebecca Fowler was a woman named Rebecca Parrot, who had been transported to the colony from England in 1656. Her indenture was then purchased by landowner Henry Cox. It was common for immigrants to work to repay the cost of transportation to the colony or to repay a debt or a criminal judgment. Logan also revealed in her research that there had been six men by the name of

Tree in St. Mary's City where the hanging of Rebecca Fowler might have occurred. *Photo by the author.*

Fowler who were transported and arrived in Maryland about the same time as Rebecca. One in particular, John Fowler, had also been transported by and indentured to Henry Cox in 1658 and is thought to be the husband of Rebecca Parrot Fowler.

Indentured servants were not allowed to marry during their terms of indenture. If Rebecca Parrot had been indentured for six years and John Fowler for four years, then they both would have been freed in 1662. After that time, Rebecca and John were eligible to marry. As newly married and freed indentured servants, John and Rebecca would have faced many challenges in Maryland, the first and foremost being earning a living.

Logan believes that John found work in Calvert County with a man by the name of George Collins, a landowner, tobacco farmer and shoemaker. It is likely that Rebecca would have worked for Collins as a domestic servant, as that was the type of work she would have done as an indentured servant. Her duties would have included housework, cooking, cleaning, laundry, childcare, healthcare and midwifery. The area of healthcare included herbal medicine and incantations or chants, which were used to bring about a positive result for the patient. Again, this practice was welcomed until and unless the outcomes were negative and involved the assistance of the devil.

Collins evidently became fond of the Fowlers, and in 1673, he gave 190 acres of land to Richard Fowler, the young son of John and Rebecca. When George Collins died in 1683, he willed to John Fowler one-third of the leather in his "tan pitt." From this, it is assumed that John also became a shoemaker. John and Rebecca evidently thrived from their work and were able to save enough money to purchase land.

In 1683, part of Prince George's County was still included in Calvert County. County land records state that John Fowler purchased a plot of land called "Fowler's Delight." John and Rebecca did not have much time to enjoy this fruit of their labors, as Rebecca was in court by 1685 and referred to as a spinster.

Rebecca's accuser, Francis Sansbury, also was an indentured servant to George Collins and still labored in that capacity when Collins died. Collins, however, did not leave anything to Sansbury in his will, which might have started some resentment toward the Fowlers. He would have been familiar with the "witchcraft" that Rebecca practiced to fulfill her role as domestic servant in the Collins household. He may have had a confrontation with her about the will situation, and she might have cursed him as a result. Then she would have been in trouble if anything injurious happened to Sansbury. Evidently, the jury believed that she attempted and succeeded in bringing about his injuries despite the fact that she was then a landowner. It is not known with certainty what the circumstances were that led to her execution, but it certainly is an interesting case.

HANNAH EDWARDS

One year later, on April 29, 1686, Hannah Edwards was indicted for witchcraft in St. Mary's County. She was a resident of Calvert County and had been delivered by the Calvert County sheriff to the St. Mary's County sheriff and charged with witchcraft. The justices of the grand jury inquest were Vincent Lowe, Henry Darnall, William Digges, William Burgess, Nicholas Sewall and Clement Hill. Darnall, Digges and Sewall are three of the same justices who were on the panel for the Rebecca Fowler inquest. Jury members were Edward Inglish (foreman), James Phillips, Samuel Cooksey, John Watson, William Aisquith, William Turner, Thomas Smithson, Benjamin Priestly, James Collyer, Cornelius Comegys,

Jacob Harriss, Benjamin Williams, William Yorke, Thomas Joce, Walter Woolverstone and Ebenezer Blackiston.

In the indictment document, Hannah was listed as the wife of Richard Edwards and as a spinster, similar to Rebecca Fowler. Here, as with Rebecca, she was presumably the widow of Richard Edwards. The document goes on to accuse Hannah of using "witchcrafts, inchantments, charmes, and sorceryes" in a felonious manner, again at Mount Calvert Hundred, as well as other locations, against Ruth Hutchinson and others, with malice and instigation of the devil. The date specified was February 6, 1685, but today the date would be the year 1686 because at that time the new year was not observed until April 1. Testimony included that their bodies were "consumed, pined, and wasted against." Hannah was subsequently arraigned for the crimes, and she pleaded not guilty to the charges.

Hannah Edwards was brought to trial on April 30, 1686, before the attorney general, Thomas Burford. The jurors for the trial were Richard Smith, Andrew Abington, Walter Lane, James Neale, John Atky, Thomas Truxton, John Allin, John Woodward, Moses Jones, Robert Benson, Thomas Price and Thomas Cooke. This jury returned a verdict of "not guilty" for the indictment for witchcraft.

Rebecca Logan's research provides additional information about Hannah Edwards. She reveals that Hannah had previously been labeled a widow but was described as married at the time of the trial. This might indicate that Rebecca Fowler, too, may have been widowed prior to her marriage to John Fowler if he was alive at the time of her trial. The same terminology is used in both legal documents. Hannah had experienced hard times prior to her trial for witchcraft, including the deaths of her stepchildren at the hands of the Indians. The Edwards couple had invested in land, a home, furniture and cattle before her indictment and trial, indicating that they were financially comfortable. Logan speculates that Ruth Hutchinson might have been an indentured servant, but there is nothing in the records to verify that. In the trial, Hannah is accused of having "consumed, pined, and wasted" the body of Hutchinson. These charges are much more vague than the "laming" charge against Rebecca Fowler, which had been apparent in the victim's physical symptoms.

Logan goes on to point out that Hutchinson was still alive twenty-three years later, so apparently the results upon her body were not so readily observed by the jury. Interestingly, two of the jurors were the same for both the Fowler and the Edwards trials. The difference in outcomes may have also had something to do with the fact that Fowler had been an indentured servant while Edwards was married to a member of the gentry. On the other hand, Fowler was not indentured at the time of trial but was convicted on the testimony of an indentured servant. Hutchinson might not have appeared credible or honest to the Edwards jury and contributed to the not guilty result.

Logan provides some additional information about Ruth Hutchinson after the trial. She was in legal trouble for committing the crime of having a child out of wedlock. She never did marry and was forced in 1704 to indenture herself to pay off her debts. Then, in 1709 she indentured her sister as a servant for five years to pay for medical care for her leg. Indenture contracts were the way that one person paid off a debt to another, but it seems strange that siblings would go through the legal process to work out a debt. The situation with her sister and the power of Ruth to indenture her is puzzling and indicates that neither of them could be trusted to settle a financial obligation. These facts lead one to the opinion that Ruth Hutchinson was a less-than-honest person and witness in court. The paradigm that guilt should be proven beyond the shadow of a doubt could have been at work for Hannah Edwards. That seems to indicate that the judicial system worked as it should have for her.

Virtue Violl

Virtue Violl was prosecuted in Maryland in 1712, much later than the other cases discussed so far and after the period of witch frenzy that pervaded the colonies at the end of the seventeenth century. At this time, the provincial capital of Maryland had been moved from St. Mary's City in St. Mary's County to Annapolis in Anne Arundel County, where it remains today. Since witchcraft was a capital offense, cases would have been heard in the provincial court, which had also moved to Annapolis.

The laws regarding witchcraft had been issued in England during the middle of the previous century, and contemporary thinking fostered skepticism regarding the existence of witches and witchcraft. The prevailing sentiment was that some innocent people had been wrongfully prosecuted, and most incidents of accusations of witchcraft were not pursued. The fact that this case was formally initiated is surprising and must have provoked a strong belief in its validity for it to go forward.

Another aspect to this case is surprising because of the logistics of the accused. Virtue Violl was a resident of Talbot County, located on the Eastern Shore of Maryland. She had to be transported across the Chesapeake Bay to Annapolis by boat. As noted in the sections about Mary Lee and Elizabeth Richardson, who were hanged at sea for being witches, there was a great suspicion and superstition regarding witches on ships and witches and water and weather. To have to travel with one who was suspected of witchcraft across the Chesapeake in a boat was dangerous for those who might have had to travel with her. The charges must have been compelling for the sheriff of Talbot County to consider the perilous journey to bring Virtue to Annapolis for the proceedings—either that or he doubted the allegations and didn't fear the journey for that reason.

On October 5, 1712, the provincial court grand jury met in Annapolis with Thomas Gassaway, sheriff, attending and Thomas Smithson, Jo Beale, Robert Bradley and Samuel Young presiding as justices. The jurors who heard the charges were John Bozman (foreman), John Taney, Notley Maddox, Edward Veazey, William Denton, Arnold Elzey, William Willoughby, William Stevens, James Monat, Henry Austin, Philemon Armstrong, Ubgate Reeves, Joseph Harrison, William Sweatnam, James Keech, Joshua Cecil, Paul Busey, Thomas Taylor, Patrick Dunkin, Thomas Tolley, Thomas Thackstone, William Gray, Jonathon Back and Thomas Price. The sheriff of Talbot County, Foster Turbutt, brought Virtue Violl into court and remanded her to the sheriff of Anne Arundel County to be held until called. The charge that they were to consider was that Virtue Violl, spinster, had diabolically used witchcraft and solicited the help of the devil to "lame and render speechless" the tongue of Elinor Moore, spinster and resident of Talbot County.

The grand jury returned an indictment against Virtue Violl, and she was held for trial. Witnesses for the trial were listed as Elinor Moore, Captain John Needles, Mrs. Needles, Robert Jadwin, Samuel Hatton and Thomas Sylvester. Jurors for the trial were Daniel Sherwood, Henry Sewall, William Veazey, Thomas Cox, Roger Laddemore, Thomas Johnson, Jonn Lanham, Phillip Kersey, Sallandine Eagle, John Houkin, Marmaduke Goodhand and Charles Jones. If testimony was given by Elinor Moore in this case, it might have been difficult for the jury to believe that she had been bewitched by Virtue Violl. In addition to that fact, if Virtue was indeed a witch, why would she not have used her power to render the other witnesses speechless so that they could not testify against her? Whatever the testimony and circumstances, the jury did acquit Virtue Violl of witchcraft on October 7, 1712.

In this case, the outcome of the witchcraft exercised by the accused could not be demonstrated if Elinor Moore testified. This would have been in contrast to the results of the Rebecca Fowler case, where the victim demonstrated that he was lamed by Rebecca's action, whether or not it was actually true.

This case was the last judicial prosecution of the crime of witchcraft in Maryland and seems to be the result of some verbal altercation between Virtue Violl and Elinor Moore. As a result of the argument, Virtue may have said that she wished that Elinor would be rendered speechless to remedy the dispute. Then Elinor probably reacted in a dramatic manner and believed that she had been cursed by Virtue. This could have been a case of hysterical paralysis as a result of the suggestion. It indicates that the entire case was probably based on an argument that transpired between two angry old maids.

Another aspect of this case is the location of the incident. The Eastern Shore of Maryland was a remote area compared to the more populated Western Shore, where the provincial capital was located. Beliefs in witchcraft were probably more firmly entrenched there than across the Chesapeake, a situation that is somewhat still true today. That part of Maryland has always been tied to the water, the Chesapeake Bay and the Atlantic Ocean. There are no large industrial cities there with sizeable populations. Fishing, tourism and farming completely dominate the culture. Maryland blue crabs, oysters and Purdue chickens are products well known from this area. Ocean City is a popular tourist destination during the summer season. The populations that support these professions are tied to the water and weather and tend to be more superstitious than those in other situations.

A search for Virtue Violl did not turn up anything about her specifically as far as a marriage or death date. The unusual name did appear in Boston, Massachusetts, during the correct period. There was a couple by the name of John and Mary Violl who had a child on September 14, 1672, and baptized their son John on September 24. When the name is spelled Viall, then there are many records of other children of John and Mary Viall. There are sons Samuel, John and Nathaniel and daughter Mary. It is possible that Virtue might have been related to this family and may have returned to Massachusetts after her trial for witchcraft in Maryland. If, in fact, she was not a native of Talbot County, that could have added to the suspicion about her by her accuser.

In all, there were a total of five criminal prosecutions of the felony and capital offense of witchcraft in Maryland. Seven cases of witchcraft have been covered in this section. Two of the seven accused witches were extrajudicially tried and executed aboard ships. The other five were prosecuted within the Provincial Court of Maryland, where felony charges with a penalty of death were held. Four of these trials took place more than ten years before the death of Moll Dyer with a guilty outcome for only one of them.

Of the five cases brought to trial, only one was a man, John Cowman, who was convicted and sentenced to hang. The sentence was revoked, and he was consequently sent to St. Mary's City to work off his obligation to the governor for an unspecified term. The only other conviction of felony witchcraft was that of Rebecca Fowler, who was sentenced and hanged as a result. All the others resulted in not guilty outcomes. Two of the cases occurred in Calvert County and one in Talbot County. Four of the trials were held in St. Mary's County, and the last one occurred in Anne Arundel County, after the colonial capital was moved to Annapolis.

These felony cases were the only five prosecuted at the provincial court level. There were many civil cases brought at the county court level regarding defamation charges by one citizen suing another over the accusation of being a witch. These cases must have brought consternation from the court officials and frustration at having to referee scores of "he said/she said" testimony from individuals suffering from the "witch paranoia" of the late seventeenth century.

One case that was investigated in 1702 involved an accusation by Charles Killburn in Anne Arundel County Court of witchcraft against Katharine Prout. On January 15, 1702, Killburn filed a complaint against Prout for practicing witchcraft and causing him to be "in a very languishing condition." He went on to explain that he would recover from his illness but then relapse after running into her and her abusive and threatening actions toward him. He said that she would wish him ill and hope that he would continue to suffer and die. Killburn asked that the court investigate the situation and possibly bring her to trial for witchcraft. She was ordered to appear before the court and behaved in a very disrespectful manner when asked to explain her actions toward Killburn. She was fined one hundred pounds of tobacco for her "saucy language." The court went on to investigate the allegation and call witnesses to testify but eventually dismissed the petition by Killburn.

Katharine Prout was not finished with the court. Charles Killburn again filed suit against Prout because he felt that she had accused him of perjury in his petition against her for witchcraft. She called him a "foresworn rogue" for his testimony in court against her. Killburn won the action with a nominal award of six pence, but he had to pay court costs of 1,101 pounds of tobacco.

Katharine Prout went on to sue a woman named Kate Quillen for defamation when she called Prout "Dame Ye," instead of "Ye Dame." That supposedly meant that she was a witch by inversion of the order of the words. Quillen accused Prout of stealing fish and molasses from a cellar in Annapolis. Prout won the suit and was awarded three pounds. This illustrates the frustration and tedium of having to listen to these cases of two women who were accusing each other of saying certain words that would defame the other. There are many such cases heard by the county court during this period.

The year 1712 saw the last known criminal prosecution of the felony of witchcraft in Maryland. Virtue Violl of Talbot County was brought to Annapolis by boat for a trial. Since there was superstition about witches that included swimming and boating, there must have been doubt in her guilt from the beginning. The "not guilty" outcome seemed to have been a foregone conclusion and the entire proceeding simply an example of the legal system "going through the motions" to meet the requirements of the law.

By 1736, Parliament had repealed the death penalty for witchcraft, and it was no longer considered a felony in England or the colonies. There must have been tremendous relief for legal officials to be rid of the frustration and aggravation of having to prosecute these cases in the colony founded on a principle of toleration.

With these legal proceedings in mind, the stage was set for the citizens of St. Mary's County to take the law into their own hands and for the legend of Moll Dyer to play out. They made decisions that determined the destiny of the county for more than three hundred years.

Part Two

FINDING MOLL DYER

Who Was Moll Dyer?

Before a detailed story about the woman who might have been Moll Dyer could be written, this question had to be answered. She had to be identified and the evidence of her existence uncovered. Once that was done, then history of the dates and locations would dictate the sequence of events that would come together to explain her life story.

The effort to identify Moll Dyer began during the summer of 2013 at the St. Mary's County Historical Society in Leonardtown, where it quickly became evident that there have been many who came there looking for records about Moll. No one had succeeded in identifying who she was or if she actually existed. The search began with accumulating copies of all the articles and stories about her that were available. Those articles revealed a list of facts that pointed to the elusive identity of the legendary witch.

This list of facts included the names of several who claimed to be related to Moll Dyer. From that list of names, the next step was construction of a family tree for each of the persons who claimed to be her relatives. Hopefully, there would be a way to connect them all and end up with a woman, common to all the trees, who could have been Moll Dyer, the legendary witch of St. Mary's County. The trees and the details of them are contained in the appendix (Genealogical Research and Family Tree Charts, Parts 1 and 2).

The legend claims that Moll Dyer was a spinster who came to America from England or Ireland with her two brothers. A premise for this search was the assumption that her name was Mary or Margaret or some variation of these names. "Moll" is a shortened version of the name Molly, which

Moll Dyer's family tree. *Original graphic illustration by artist Julie Cowdery, Surratt House Museum.*

is a term of endearment for the proper names of Mary or Margaret. Therefore, the prize was a woman named Mary or Margaret Dyer who had two brothers and was related to all the claimants, the appropriate age and never married.

Family trees were done for Sarah Frances Dyer Mudd, Reverend Edward Dyer, Mary Magdalene Dyer Simms, Marie "Mattie" Dyer Purcell and William Kane. Their roots all led back to Devon, England, and a woman named Mary Dyer, who was born in 1634. How did she start in England and end up in St. Mary's County, Maryland?

Records revealed the trail of Mary and her brothers as they left Bristol, England, and traveled to the West Indies as indentured servants. From there, they each made their ways to America and Maryland, as ship records showed. Mary and her brother William both became residents of Maryland, Mary in St. Mary's County and William in Charles County. For the detailed chronology and documentation of this journey, consult the appendix.

After many months of tracking these records, the conclusion is that Mary Dyer, born in 1634 in Devon, England, to William Dyer and Elizabeth Holcombe, is the legendary witch of St. Mary's County, Moll Dyer. The records show her baptism and her immigration to Maryland in 1677 with her brothers William and Edward (and relative Thomas), via the Nevis Plantation indentures in 1669. There is no record of her marriage or death, making her an elderly spinster in St. Mary's County in 1697. She learned about "witchcraft" (herbal remedies, spells and voodoo) while at Nevis Plantation and brought that knowledge with her. She continued as an indigent resident on the land known as St. Margaret's in St. Mary's County until her death in 1697. Knowing her identity and the sequence of events allows the story of her life to wind itself among the facts uncovered.

Moll's Story

From those facts about Mary Dyer (b. 1634) revealed by the investigation in the preceding chapter and detailed in the appendix, the complete story of Mary as she became the witch Moll Dyer of St. Mary's County needs to be told. The historical events in Devon, England, St. Kitts, the West Indies and St. Mary's County revealed the possibilities of the life that she led. She existed and has been identified. The following narrative will help to fill the gaps in her life story based on history to reveal details about the life of any poor, independent woman during the seventeenth century. The realm of possibility allows the following story to emerge.

On a cold February day in 1634, William and Elizabeth brought another daughter into the bleak world of Kenn, Devon, England. Mary was the fourth child of William Dyer and Elizabeth Holcombe and the third daughter; at that time, they also had Thomas (born in 1625), Agnes (1629) and Dorothy (1632). They went on to have a total of seven children, five of whom were daughters. William was born in 1635, Elizabeth in 1638 and Christian in 1641.[12] Mary was the middle child and just another burden to her parents during a period in history when civil war raged in England and hard times were visited on the population trying to deal with the results of that turmoil.

When little Mary was eight years old, in 1642, the civil war between Parliament and King Charles I began and brought many years of strife and turmoil to the country, Devon and the Dyers. Since Thomas was the oldest, seventeen when the war started, it is possible that he was called to fight during the war, which lasted until 1646, when he would have been twenty-one. Mary would have been just twelve when the first war ended. Parliament took over the governing of England with the surrender of Charles I, and Devon was in the midst of change, financial strife and devastation. Money was scarce, along with young men who had survived the fighting, but Thomas was not killed and lived until 1690.

War was not over, though, and the Royalists who wanted to return Charles I to the throne began fighting anew in 1648. Mary was fourteen when the second civil war began and just entering young womanhood when many of the young men went away to fight and never returned. Charles I was beheaded in 1649, but the Royalists fought on to secure the throne for Charles II. It was not until 1660 that he was restored to the throne of England. During that period, the Dutch-Anglo Wars were also fought, and the governance of England was in a constant state of change as Cromwell and the military waged a constant effort to take charge.

During this most turbulent period for Devon and the Dyers, Mary's brother William married his wife, Agnes Thorne, and they had a son named William, who was born in 1657. Mary's sister Dorothy was married on February 17, 1655, to Thomas Hawkins, and they had a child almost every year thereafter. With her nephew William's birth and the subsequent births of her nieces and nephews, Mary would have been busy along with her mother, Elizabeth, helping with the deliveries of the babies and assisting with the care of the children. She most likely would have found employment in the township doing domestic work for the residents who had money to pay for help. The income that she could earn was necessary to support her large family. She also would have learned herbal medicine alongside her mother as she worked to help support her family and take care of her nieces and nephews as that number steadily increased.

Domestic duties included cooking, sewing, cleaning, farming, nursing, midwifery and healing illness for members of the family, her own and any other families with whom she would have sought employment. These skills were necessary for women who were destined to be wives, mothers or domestic servants, the common profession for single women of the working class in England during this period.

Dorothy and Thomas had son John in 1656, son William in 1658, son Thomas in 1659, daughter Dorothy in 1661, son Richard who was born and died in 1665, daughter Elizabeth in 1666, son Christopher in 1667 and finally daughter Jane in 1671. Jane was born after Mary left Devon in 1669 with her brother William to head for the American colonies in search of a better life. There was not much of a future for them in Devon.

It is possible that Mary married a man named Richard Northcutt on September 23, 1657, when she was twenty-three years old, as there is a record of a marriage in Devon between Mary Dyer and Richard Northcutt. However, Mary Dyer is a common name in England, and it may have been another woman by that name. Another possibility is that Mary did marry Richard and that he was killed during the fighting shortly thereafter so that she did not ever change her name to Northcutt and just went forward as she had been doing prior to the marriage. At any rate, there is no further record of them as a couple or of him as a husband. If she did marry, it did not serve to help her situation and just made her a widow with no money who needed to find another husband.

By the end of the wars, Mary was twenty-six years old at a time when men were scarce and money for a dowry was almost impossible to procure. Only the very wealthy were negotiating marriages; the working classes found very few matches. The rules for marriage were complicated, including the required dowry, if a suitor for a daughter could be found. The Dyers did manage to marry off two of their daughters, Dorothy and Christian. Christian, however, was not married until much later, February 26, 1684, at age forty-two, to Edward Watts, not alleviating the financial burden on the family during the war years. Christian died shortly after her marriage, possibly in bearing her first child.

More wars and plague were in store for the people of Devon during the 1660s and for the Dyers as Mary continued to age unmarried. By the time 1669 arrived in Devon, plague and war had become the norm. The ravages of war, poverty and disease in England made the change of residence an appealing alternative to the extremely difficult life in Devon. Mary was thirty-five years old, unmarried or widowed, and any prospect of marriage had disappeared for her there. In contrast, women were in demand in the colonies, and maybe she could find a suitable match if she could survive the trip and the elements in the New World.

The year 1669 was a milestone for Mary Dyer and her younger brother, William. Promise of a better life, riches and wealth perpetuated by the rich owner-planters of land in the West Indies lured many of the downtrodden, war-weary and poverty-stricken working-class citizens of England to indenture themselves for passage, work and board to the owners of sugar plantations in the islands. Political prisoners and prisoners of war were also shipped to these plantations as indentured servants by the ruling regime at the time. William and Mary were two of those who bought the dream and signed up to leave war-torn Devon for the New World. They traveled to Bristol, England, where they boarded ships bound for Nevis Plantation on St. Kitts Island in the West Indies. Mary left on October 25, bound to Thomas Lugg for a period of four years as an indentured servant. Later, on December 3, William departed from Bristol bound to William Salter, also on Nevis Plantation, St. Kitts, West Indies, for a period of four years. Thus the adventure began for them.

Crossing the Atlantic was not easy on passengers, especially the indentured servants. There was sickness, bad weather and mistreatment at the hands of the ship's captain and crew to endure. It was not an undertaking for the weak of spirit or body to cross the ocean at that time. The conditions within the confines of the ship's hold were filthy, and food had to be preserved for lengthy journeys across the Atlantic. Passengers had to endure the hardships of sea travel along with the seasonal storms and spoiling food. It is miraculous that so many survived that ordeal to arrive at their destinations. Mary would have traveled during hurricane season, while William had to weather the freezing temperatures of the winter. They both managed to arrive in St. Kitts in condition to begin the hardships of the indentured servants on sugar plantations for a period of four years.

Mary arrived in St. Kitts before William, who arrived there in early 1670. At that time, the English and Dutch had been fighting over the rights to the West Indies largely because of the riches to be had from the growing and harvesting of sugar cane. The cane was processed there into sugar that was used to manufacture rum. The sugar, rum and slave trade was lucrative; thus, the two countries continually struggled for control of individual islands and sugar plantations. The English and Dutch wanted to dominate the trade and fought each other between 1654 and 1674, so war continued as Mary and William began their indentures to their respective masters on Nevis.

Indentured servants swarmed to the West Indies during the English Civil War as people fled the war, poverty and disease that plagued that country. England also exported the opposition members as prisoners as each side gained control, so the indentured population of the island rose until slaves were found in Africa and exported to the islands to work the sugar plantations. They worked for their entire lives after being purchased and eliminated the need for the owners to pay and maintain the indentured servants for limited terms of service. During the 1670s, the slave population steadily grew, while the white indentured population numbers fell. The difficult work harvesting the cane and boiling it in the tropical heat was better tolerated by the slaves who had come there from similar climate conditions in Africa.

The weather in the West Indies was extremely difficult for the English planters and their families who came there to make their fortunes. The heat, along with the insects and disease, made life for them unbearable at times. Many of the families gave it up and returned to England, especially as the diseases began to claim many lives of the fragile women and children. An unusual ability of the "Caribs," as the English referred to the native Caribbeans, to forecast hurricanes by observing rings around the moon precipitated rumors of witchcraft among the English when the forecasts came true. One such hurricane hit St. Kitts in 1669 right before Mary and William arrived there.

The English planters brought their lifestyle to the islands, including churches, magistrates and political institutions. They established society as they had known it, a culture that revolved around the presence of servants, including indentured servants and African slaves. The planter class depended on the slave community for their livelihood as well as their very existence. The slaves were much better adapted to the conditions than the English plantation owners and were able to take care of the planter families very effectively.

Conditions for the indentured servants were the same as those for the slaves. They were provided the bare minimum for living: living quarters, food and clothing. They lived together with the slaves, sharing their destinies during the time of their indentures, usually four or five years. Mary spent a total of eight years there, probably to earn her passage to continue to America. The first four years paid for her to travel to St. Kitts from England. The women worked at domestic chores while the men worked the sugar cane fields. The slaves, of course, were there for life.

There were laws and rules that governed the treatment of slaves and indentured servants by English law. The Code of 1661[13] was drawn up and provided the following requirements for each:

The Code of 1661

	SLAVES	INDENTURED SERVANTS
Food	none	Minimum Allotments
Clothing	1 Year (male - 1 cap, 1 drawers; female - 1 cap, 1 petticoat)	Minimum Allotments

	SLAVES	INDENTURED SERVANTS
Discipline	Whatever the owner determined	Owner sued for mistreatment or charged with murder
Punishment	Whipping, branding, nose slitting for capital crimes (murder, rape, arson, assault, theft > 1 shilling) determined by 2 justices of the peace and 3 freeholders	Extra years of servitude: (jury trial) 1 year - assaulting master 2 years - theft 3 years - impregnating servant, running away 7 years - harboring fugitive slave

Thus the law provided protection of some sort for this part of the population. Mary began her eight years at Nevis alongside the slaves who worked at domestic chores for Thomas Lugg, who had contracted for her indenture before she left Bristol. She would have shared her skills learned working in Devon, and the slaves would have shared with her the customs and rituals from the cultures from which they came. Surely, the cooking, herbal remedies, midwifery and practices of the local religions would have been a part of the lessons that Mary learned, and that might have included voodoo and other practices to bring about both good and bad results.

Two of the African belief systems that predominated then and still exist today are Obeahism and Myalism. Both include occult practices, handed down generations-old techniques for curing illness with herbs and plants, as well as rituals that were invoked to bring about beneficial results. Society would have labeled this as witchcraft, but as long as the results were successful in curing illness, they would have been considered good witchcraft or "white magic." These practices were the norm in Nevis and barely one step away from a visit with a doctor. Medical practitioners were scarce to start with, and even if one could be found, the approach to curing illness was not that far from the witchcraft of the local self-trained domestics and midwives.

Along with the African witchcraft and healing techniques, Moll would have added the treatments, including herbs and spells, that she had learned in Devon to increase her value to the planter's household. She would have cooked for the family and the working slaves, cleaned the house and taken care of the children as part of her duties. When they became sick, she would have used her herbs and spiritual routines to try to cure them. When the women of the house delivered babies, Moll would have been there to help bring their babies into the world. Thus was the world of domestic servants, one in which Moll was probably proficient by her fortieth year in 1674.

Disease was rampant given filthy living conditions, contaminated food and water and a multitude of insects and vermin contributing to a vile existence in Nevis. Some of the diseases that were predominant in Nevis were malaria, yellow fever, tuberculosis, venereal disease, dysentery, dropsy, leprosy, hookworm, yaws (skin ulcers), elephantiasis, sleeping sickness and Guinea worm disease. Some of the therapies to cure these diseases used turtle pee (dried, powdered and mixed with beer or wine) and goose dung. Doctors who practiced at that time believed in four "humors" in the body, those being melancholy, phlegm, blood and choler, all of which needed to be in balance for good health. They used herbal nostrums to achieve the balance needed by the body, and bloodletting was a common cure for almost every ailment. The local witch or domestic healer would have been an attractive alternative to being subjected to the methods of the closest physician, especially if the domestic witchery had achieved some successful outcomes.

Often the medicinal approaches by the slaves from Africa were preferable and more humane than the European methods employed by white doctors, even if one happened to be available. In Williamsburg, Virginia, a wealthy plantation owner and doctor named Landon Carter owned a slave named Nassau who had intervened and saved the life of a young colonial girl. This girl, named Franky, had been sent to the slave hospital to be exposed to measles and became ill with the disease. Nassau prevented a bloodletting procedure because he thought her pulse too weak to survive it. In his diary, Carter wrote:

> *This was probably not the only time Nassau, or any other slave caring for the sick, contravened European medical practice—and his master. Like most Africans, Nassau understood herbal and folk medicine and perhaps saw the uselessness of draining blood from sick people. Folk practitioners like Nassau probably did more good—or at least less harm—than white doctors practicing European-style medicine.*[14]

Around the same time, a clergyman named Samuel Parris brought two native slaves named John and Tituba from Barbados with him to Salem Village, Massachusetts. John concocted a "witch cake" to accompany Tituba's incantations when they treated illness there, and their partnership (which obviously didn't result in success) and her testimony were largely responsible for the Salem witchcraft frenzy in 1692. In this instance, the slave knowledge of witchcraft was used to identify and prosecute white witches.

In 1674, Mary's brother William arrived in Virginia from the West Indies; he proceeded to Maryland and settled in Prince George's County. He also brought his wife, Agnes, and son William from Devon to join him in the Maryland Colony. Son William married Joan Lane, who also lived in Prince George's County, and had a son named Patrick Dyer. These Dyers and their descendants can be seen in Tree Diagram—part 1 shown in the appendix.

Mary "Moll" Dyer may have remained with Steven Lugg for all eight years of her indenture or moved on to another planter and a different island, but she did not immigrate to America until 1677, when she arrived in Dorchester County, Maryland. A curious fact about her arrival in Maryland was that there were three women named Dyer on the ship that brought her there. They were listed as Mary, Margaret and Molligo, all variations of the same name. It is possible that Mary had acquired the nickname of Molligo from her slave associates at Nevis, some of whom could have been on that ship and called her that. Consequently, all three of the named passengers on that ship were most likely the same woman who eventually became known as "Moll" Dyer.

After Mary's arrival, she proceeded to St. Mary's County, probably because she had secured an indenture contract to work for a citizen in the St. Margaret's area of Newtowne Hundred, now known as Leonardtown. Most likely, William had worked to secure that position for his sister before her arrival on the Eastern Shore of Maryland. In return for her services, she was given a parcel of land on which to reside. There she remained, close to her brother, until her death in 1697.

For twenty years, Mary "Moll" lived and worked in the Newtowne area. When she arrived, she was forty-three years old; she died at sixty-three. She probably started off as an indentured servant until she worked through her contract. When she was free to go and do as she wanted, she remained in the area and continued to live on the land where she had established her home, probably as a tenant of her former master. She supported herself doing what she had been doing all of her adult life: domestic service and herbal medicine, including midwifery and good witchcraft. As she aged and the universal paranoia about witchcraft developed in Massachusetts, local people became more focused on the outcomes of her efforts and specifically when those outcomes were not the results that they wanted. She was an old spinster Catholic woman who practiced witchcraft and even more unusual African rituals that she brought with her from the West Indies. These facts added up to score against her when bad luck entered the scenario. Moll had many tools in her medical bag as a result of her time in Nevis. In addition, just surviving her stay there probably gave her some level of immunity to many of the diseases that she had been exposed to while there.

Moll lived in a small hut in the woods and grew her own herbs, vegetables and flowers, which she used for her medicine and incantations or spells. She also had goats, chickens, pigs and maybe a cow to sustain herself. The practice of witchcraft during this period in America and Europe was a normal part of life. It was no problem for anyone as long as the results were beneficial to the customers of the given witch. All of the strange rituals and brews were fine as long as they helped those who sought out the witch for assistance. When the results turned negative, the people looked to the persecution of witches for resolution of the problems that they felt that she/he had caused. To be called a witch wasn't a derogatory label until and unless it was in conjunction with the combination of devil worship and negative outcomes. Recipe books from the seventeenth century support this fact, since they contain these herbal recipes and remedies and even a few prayers and rituals.

The legal definition of witchcraft that was used within the 1690s and referred to devil worship was complicated and measured by compliance with a list of criteria from the legal perspective. Keep in mind that the same behavior that was evident with positive outcomes becomes a crime when the outcomes have negative intent. The same legal process for prosecuting witchcraft was prevalent in both Europe and America during the late 1600s. While witches could pursue fortune-telling, herbalism and faith-healing with humans and animals with impunity, they became objects of persecution when their efforts invoked devil worship and caused illness, death and disasters such as extreme weather and crop failure. This activity could also include familiars such as cats, dogs, goats, toads or any animal that might be invisible. The key to determining whether or not a woman was practicing witchcraft was the invocation of the devil to produce the results of her efforts. That was a very difficult aspect to prove and led to the dismissal of many attempts to prosecute a witch. Witches who were prosecuted were generally unmarried and elderly Catholic women, generally as a result of the Puritan influence in society at that time.

The general persecution of Catholics in England when the Church of England dominated contributed to the widespread suspicion and distrust of Catholicism and the rituals of the church. That led to the road of prosecution of witchcraft as a crime in England and in the colonies. The predominance

Replica of a typical slave or indentured servant hut in St. Mary's City. *Photo by the author.*

of Catholicism in the Maryland Colony, along with the founding paradigm of religious tolerance, would seem to be a contradiction in Maryland to the facts of the witch trials.

As the winter of 1697 approached in St. Mary's County, there were a series of unfortunate events that occurred in the area in general and to Moll's medical practice in particular. The legend includes a story about the death of a young girl who had been in the care of Moll Dyer, a death that had been completely unexpected and for which the parents held Moll responsible. That, in itself, was not sufficient to indict Moll for witchcraft or to lead to her persecution or prosecution by the neighborhood. From that event, a series of hardships began that led the populace to begin to suspect the witch of casting some bad spells on the area. The crops had failed that fall, and there had been a larger than usual number of farm animal deaths. These unfortunate situations were probably the result of hot and/or dry weather, with the crop failure leading to the deaths of the animals.

When the depth of the winter was in full force, the temperatures fell to record lows and killed more livestock, while an outbreak of influenza began killing off a large number of the populace. It was an extremely harsh winter. In fact, on March 27, 1697, the Council of Maryland proceedings commented:

> It hath pleased God that this winter hath been the longest that hath been known in the memory of man, for it began about the middle of November, and little sign of any spring yet. It was very uncertain weather, several frosts and snows, one of which was the greatest hath been known.

As the series of unfortunate events continued, the people needed to explain the apparent bad luck and began to fear that Moll Dyer had been practicing evil witchcraft. She began to fear the wrath of her neighbors as their anger increased. When the neighbors saw that Moll seemed to be unaffected by the elements that plagued them, they directed their anger and frustration toward her in their language and actions. To keep her angry neighbors away, it is likely that she began to try to scare them from harassing her by casting some spells when they would approach her. The aggravation went both ways and escalated to the point of each side living in fear of the other for no real reason. This fear led to the dire consequences that followed.

Given the results of the legal proceedings of the previous witch trials in Maryland, the probability of a guilty outcome for similar action against Moll was very slim. The citizens of St. Mary's County, who were the neighbors of Moll Dyer in Newtowne and Poplar Hill, should be considered in the time and context of these circumstances. They must have considered several options about how to take care of the problems that they faced.

First of all, they knew they were in a dire situation. All their problems were ultimately caused by the weather, a supernatural phenomenon to them. From their experience, there had to be something diabolical at work because there was no other possibility for them. It had to be the work of a witch.

Who was the local witch? Moll Dyer. From the facts, her neighbors must have discussed their possible options. They could try to get the local sheriff to arrest Moll and charge her with witchcraft. First, the sheriff was occupied outside the county in a rebellion in Baltimore. If residents could find some official to arrest her, they could attempt to bring her to trial for the specifics of witchcraft as defined by law. They would need a victim who could demonstrate some physical manifestation of the alleged curse, like lameness in the case of Rebecca Fowler. That was not the situation. Moll's curse would have had to do with the weather. The only weather-related witch proceedings had occurred on the ships outside of the judicial process.

Then, they would have had to speculate on the outcome of the proceedings. Without a victim with physical symptoms, she would have probably been found not guilty and allowed to live as she had before the accusations. That would not have solved the problem. The other outcome, which is what they would have sought, would have been a guilty verdict and execution by hanging. It is not likely that the people who lived around Moll Dyer wanted to see her hanged. They were people who came to Maryland to enjoy the atmosphere of religious tolerance, as stated in the charter for the colony. They simply wanted to get rid of the problem to bring relief to the area. They wanted her to go away and leave them alone. Consequently, they took matters into their own hands.

Burning Moll Dyer's hut seemed to be the most efficient way of forcing her to leave the area. That is what the locals decided to do and did on that very cold night.

Those citizens who approached Moll's hut late that night didn't intend to harm her, just force her to leave the area and consequently leave them alone. They didn't consider that she could not go far on foot and that she would have been angry at them after that.

Late in the night, Moll's neighbors approached her little hut in the woods. The torches they carried helped to light their way and keep them warm as the temperatures plunged to dangerous lows on that record cold winter night. She slept as they tossed their torches onto the roof and through the windows of her house. When she awoke, the fire in her small house was raging throughout, and she quickly grabbed the blanket under which she slept to wrap around her body. She found her way outside and realized that the angry group had set the fire. She feared for her life and raced away from the fire and her angry neighbors. Her only thought was that they were intent on killing her as she ran over the frozen ground in her bare and freezing feet. As the glow of the fire burning down her hut illuminated the woods and warmed the angry persecutors, Moll found herself slowly freezing in her nightgown with only a blanket to keep her warm. As the dark and cold engulfed her, she realized that she was losing her battle to stay warm. Knowing that she would quickly die, she climbed on top of a fieldstone she found to try to keep her body off the frozen ground. As the darkness of death overcame her, she knelt on the rock and stretched her arm toward heaven, praying that God would save her and condemning the actions of her neighbors for burning her house.

Relieved that they had driven Moll away and removed the source of the adverse witchcraft, they had no idea of the results of their actions as far as Moll's actual fate. It was not until a few days later that a local boy found Moll's body frozen on the stone as he searched for some lost animals in the woods. He ran from the woods to his family farm nearby with the news of the body he had discovered. His relatives and neighbors went back into the woods with him to retrieve the frozen body and bury it in the local indigents' cemetery near the shore of the Breton Bay inlet close by. Somehow, they knew that what they had done was wrong, but they were glad that the area populace would not have to worry about any more bad witchcraft on the part of Moll Dyer. Or would they?

Some of those who had helped bring her body out of the frozen woods shared the view they had of her posture reaching heavenward and assumed that she had cursed the people who had done this to her. They also assumed that she had cursed the entire area and not just the people who had done the deed when difficult times continued for the land and the county thereafter. Could they have suffered from a mass hysteria of guilt after the mob murder of this poor old woman?

Regardless of the reason, St. Mary's County continued to suffer hard times after the surreptitious death of the feared and hated witch Moll Dyer. Although she was not there to invoke spells and curses on the area, the consequential bad luck that the area continued to experience was attributed to the curse that she had invoked as she froze to death that night. The story lived on, retold time and time again to subsequent generations of residents of St. Mary's County. Whether or not she was a witch is a question that needs no answer. Her continued influence over the attitudes of the people of the area speaks volumes to the extent of her power, either by intention on her part or guilt on the part of her fellow residents.

Enough ill consequences occur around the famous rock and the Moll Dyer area to at least make people wonder about the suspected curse and fuel the legend even today. There have been reports of strange weather events that have happened when residents of the area have braved the woods and followed the Moll Dyer Run. The local lore reports apparitions of a white dog and headless horse that appear in the area. The ghost of Moll herself is supposed to appear annually on the coldest night of the year and make appearances at other times with the ghost of the white dog. These visions have been reported to have caused automobile accidents near the Moll Dyer Road intersection with Maryland Route 5 or Point Lookout Road. The rock itself, located in Leonardtown, is reported to cause strange incidents. Illness, accidents and camera failures seem to occur after contact with the boulder.

No matter the facts, the stories have lived on for 320 years. The belief that Moll Dyer lived and died in these woods has brought the population of St.

Moll Dyer flees her persecutors. *Original illustration by artist Bonnie W. Glod.*

Mary's County to at least acknowledge the possibility that any of it is true. There must be a shred of truth in the legend given it has lasted this long. If it was just a story, it likely would have died out long ago.

Moll Dyer was born in a century when women had no voice, no rights and no options except at the discretion of a man. Her best hope of any autonomy was as a widow. Mary did not marry. She traveled from England to the West Indies alone on ships where the numbers of deaths were very high. She lived on a sugar plantation with slaves for eight years and took care of people who were sick with various illnesses. She traveled to Maryland alone and lived alone for twenty years while supporting herself and surviving the elements and more illnesses, again while taking care of her neighbors in their times of need and sickness. She was a strong, independent woman, which made her the target of "witch hunters" when that crime was a popular explanation for any woman who was different—and different she was, for sure. She should have been respected for being able to survive in a time when survival was the exception and not the rule.

6

Whodunit

Now that the story of what happened to Mary Dyer is known, and the tragic series of events that led to her death as the legendary witch known as Moll Dyer have unfolded in St. Mary's County, the next step to understanding the reasons for what happened is to look at who might have been responsible. To find out who they were is part of the story. The other part is the stories of their families and the circumstances and challenges that they faced. Only then will the entire picture be clear and reveal how the legend was born and survived for more than three centuries. Imagine the obstacles to survival these people faced in the middle of the seventeenth century at the start of civilized society in a strange and undeveloped location known as the colony of Maryland in the new land, America. Only the strong of body and spirit could conquer the elements, disease and conflicts with the Native Americans that claimed 80 percent of the colonists. They were prepared to fight whatever they faced, including evil witchcraft directed at them.

First, to find the residents in question, knowledge of the local geography of the state is necessary. Maryland was divided into seven counties: Anne Arundel, Calvert, Charles, Kent, St. Mary's, Somerset and Talbot. The counties of Maryland were divided into parcels called "Hundreds" when the original land grants were made by King Charles of England. Newtowne Hundred was the location where Moll Dyer lived and where Leonardtown, Moll Dyer Road and Moll Dyer Run are found today. The parcel located directly adjacent to Newtowne was Poplar Hill Hundred and where more

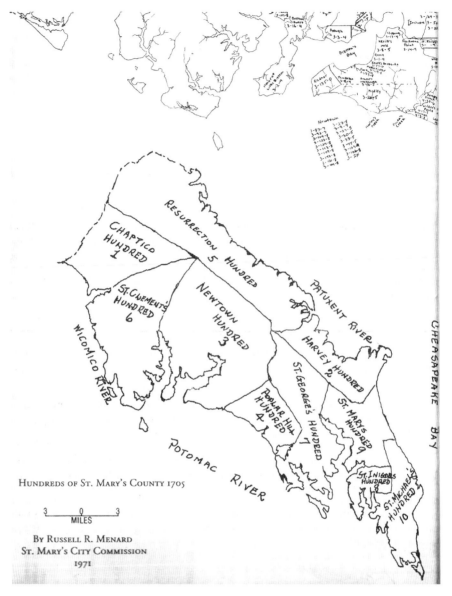

Hand-drawn map of St. Mary's County "Hundreds" as of 1705. *St. Mary's County Historical Society "Chronicles of St. Mary's."*

of Moll's neighbors would have lived in 1697. Those two divisions of the county are the focus of this research, and their residents are the possible participants in the Moll Dyer incident.

The citizens of Newtowne and Poplar Hill Hundreds were struggling just to carve out a subsistent existence in the wilderness of the New World that fall of 1697. They were farming their land, fishing the waters of the Potomac, Patuxent and St. Mary's Rivers and the Chesapeake Bay. They simply wanted a bountiful harvest and a healthy existence while they were free to practice whatever religion they chose. After all, Maryland's charter was based on religious tolerance. Colonists welcomed all to this area, including Catholics, Protestants, Quakers and others, even benevolent "witches" who used their knowledge to heal the sick, deliver babies or produce a bountiful crop. They could never have anticipated the severe weather that beset them or the devastating results that such weather could bring. They were not prepared to deal with the subsequent rampant illness and death visited on them that fall and winter.

The residents of the area had not experienced such harsh conditions since coming to the New World, and they did not understand why God had suddenly made things so difficult for them. Even the legislators in Annapolis made remarks in the records regarding the severity of the winter. It must have been a result of some spell or curse invoked by a witch. At least, that was the way they began to explain it. After all, the fall had been unusually wet and caused the corn and tobacco crops to mold and fail. Then the winter temperatures plummeted to unheard of low levels and brought about the death of large numbers of the cattle and other farm animals. When an influenza epidemic broke out and brought about the deaths of so many, the people began to question the motives of the local witch, Moll Dyer.

By 1697, Moll had lived in her hut for about twenty years. She had spent her life using her witchcraft to bring health and positive results for her neighbors during that time. Occasionally, she lost a child or a patient in childbirth, but that was normal for that time. Doctors, if and when they were available, hardly had any more success using many of the same methods or the harsher techniques used by the medical profession. Moll grew her herbs and raised her goats, pigs and cattle to sell products made from them to her clients whenever they visited her for remedies.

Life was good for Moll, a sixty-three-year-old spinster who had survived her journeys and exposure to illnesses in England, ocean voyages and the West Indies over her lifetime. Spinsterhood also contributed to her well-being and longevity. She did not have to deal with the closeness of having a husband and children, who would have spread illnesses and jeopardized her health over the years. Not having to deal with and survive producing a child every year was key to her longevity. Childbirth was the single largest threat to the lives of women throughout the seventeenth century. Living alone in the woods worked out well for her life plan—that was, until the winter of 1697.

Moll's neighbors could not understand how the circumstances that were severely affecting their lives weren't having an impact on the local witch, or maybe they did. After all, she was a witch. She must have been cursing the local area and populace and causing the weather to wreak havoc on their lives. They were landowners and tenants who farmed vast fields of tobacco, which was the currency of the time. When the crop failed, they were financially ruined. This witch was responsible for their suffering, death and financial ruin. She had to go immediately. They did not want the complications and delay of trying to charge Moll with witchcraft in the courts. Neither did they want to deal with the most likely outcome of a trial, which was a "not guilty" verdict. They just wanted her gone and her curse on the area to be removed. Thus, a group of her neighbors decided that the best way to rid themselves of her wrath was to burn her hut and force her to leave.

Who exactly were those neighbors who descended on Moll that night and burned her hut? Did their descendants remain residents of St. Mary's County until the present time? Do they believe today that their families were cursed as everyone believed?

Land records of early Maryland revealed the names of landowners, parcel titles and purchase dates prior to 1697 in St. Mary's County. After reviewing nine hundred pages of records, a list emerged with about three hundred names of landowners in St. Mary's County.[15] From there, the 1705 map listed the index of names of owners and parcels contained in each Hundred. These parcels were divisions of the Hundred and sold or granted to individuals who came to the colony, and the size was based on the number of people that the prospective landowner transported there with him. Newtowne and Poplar Hill were the two closest Hundreds to the land where Moll Dyer lived. That index revealed about one hundred of the original three hundred who lived in those two parcels.[16]

The tax records contained more information about any tenants (renters) or "possessors" of the land parcels in question.[17] With that information, the Dr. Lois Green Carr Career File Collection at the Maryland State Archives revealed the biographies of the residents of St. Mary's County in the seventeenth and eighteenth centuries. From the biological facts, such as birth and death dates, the list was narrowed to "The Dirty Thirty," or those who were candidates based on their circumstances or proximity. From those thirty names and further study of genealogical records and the Carr narratives, the list was reduced to the "Ten Most Likely." Those ten are possibly the ones who were involved in the burning that night and bear closer scrutiny.

The Dirty Thirty

Owner	Description	Acres	Acquire Date	Location	Possessor	Primary
Ashman, Richard	Ashman's Freehold	150	01 Jan 1666	Newtowne		PH
Banks, Richard	Dunbar	100	01 Jan 1648	Poplar Hill		LJB
Banks, Richard & Wright, William	Poplar Hill	200	01 Jan 1641	Poplar Hill		LJB
Bayley/ Bailey, John	Bayley's Rest/ Small Hope	350	24 Aug 1694	Newtowne	Waters, Joseph	PH
Bell, Daniel	Hopewell	200	06 May 1686	Poplar Hill		LJB
Bennet, Richard	Bennet/ Tunnel	200	01 Jan 1651	Poplar Hill		LJB
Brown, William & Thimbleby, John	Honest Tom's Inheritance	150	01 Jan 1649	Newtowne	Thomas, Robert	PH
Campbell, John	Oyster Shell Neck	50	01 Jan 1666	Poplar Hill		LJB
Campbell, John	Gravelly Hill	50	01 Jan 1662	Poplar Hill		LJB
Campbell, John	Outlet	100	01 Jan 1662	Poplar Hill		LJB
Campbell, John	Fox Hill	30	01 Jan 1662	Poplar Hill		LJB

Owner	Description	Acres	Acquire Date	Location	Possessor	Primary
Clark, Robert	St. Lawrence Freehold	100	01 Jan 1652	Newtowne		PH, LJB
Cole, Robert	Cole's Addition	50	10 Jun 1686	Newtowne	Bloomfield, James	PH
Drury, Robert	Dry Dockin Addition	100	20 Oct 1683	Newtowne	Tant, James	PH, LJB
Fosse, John	Shocke Park	100	15 Feb 1683	Newtowne		PH
Hagon, Thomas	Cadock Measure	150	01 Jan 1672	Newtowne		PH, LJB
Hall, Walter	Revell's Backside	100	01 Jan 1663	Newtowne		PH, LJB
Hammond, Daniel & John	Lewgar's Plains	430	01 Jul 1682	Newtowne	Norris, John	PH, LJB
Hammond, Mordeca	St. Bernard's	100	01 Jan 1664	Newtowne	Joseph, James	PH
Heard/ Hurd, John	Heard's Choice	150	22 Oct 1681	Newtowne	Widow Susanna Heard	LJB
Heard/ Hurd, John	Coventry/ Offley	100/ 180	19 Oct 1680	Newtowne	Widow Susanna Heard	LJB
Johnson, James	Latchford	200	01 Jan 1647	Poplar Hill		LJB
Lewger, John	Philip's Purchase	100	01 Jan 1658	Newtowne	Cecil, Thomas	PH
Medley, John	Medley/ Pococomoco Point	1250	01 Jan 1651	Newtowne		PH
Nevitt, Richard	Nevet's/St. Ann's	100	01 Jan 1653	Newtowne		LJB
Obryan, Mathias	Scotland/ Bryon/Green Meadows	100/ 100	01 Jan 1651	Newtowne		LJB

Owner	Description	Acres	Acquire Date	Location	Possessor	Primary
Pakes, Walter	St. Anne/ Peter's Hill	100	01 Jan 1649	Newtowne	Jarbo, Henry	PH, LJB
Pakes, Walter	St. Francis	500	01 Jan 1665	Newtowne	Jarbo, Henry	PH, LJB
Pakes, Walter	St. Margaret's	300	01 Jan 1666	Newtowne	Gough, James	PH, LJB
Revell, Randall	Revell	300	01 Jan 1641	Newtowne		LJB
Salmon, Thomas	Rochester/ The Poole	200/ 120	01 Jan 1672	Newtowne	Greenwell, James	PH
Simpson, Paul	Crackbourne's Purchase	200	01 Jan 1652	Newtowne	Cooper, Thomas	PH
Smith, Capt. Henry	Smith's Rest	100	05 Oct 1695	Poplar Hill		LJB
Smith, Daniel	Smith's Rest	35	08 Aug 1694	Poplar Hill		LJB
Tant/ Taunt, John	Taunton Deane	40	14 Dec 1683	Newtowne		LJB
Tant/ Taunt, John	Tant/Taunt's Mark	160	14 Dec 1683	Newtowne	Widow	LJB
Taylor, Frances	Fortune	50	19 Oct 1684	Newtowne	Tant, John	PH
Taylor, Henry	Kingstown	50	01 Jan 1670	Newtowne	Fosse, John	PH, LJB
Tennihill, William	Marking Place	100	01 Jan 1666	Poplar Hill		LJB
Thompson, Arthur	Hownestow	100	01 Jan 1674	Newtowne	Farthing, William	LJB
Thompson, Arthur	St. Osward	200	07 May 1683	Newtowne	Bayley, John	LJB
Thompson, Arthur	Hampstead	200	26 Jan 1683	Newtowne		LJB
Thompson, Robert	Hard Fortune	100	05 Oct 1695	Newtowne	Thompson, James	LJB

Owner	Description	Acres	Acquire Date	Location	Possessor	Primary
Thompson, William	Indian Quarter/ Koaxe's	250	01 Jan 1648	Newtowne	Brooks, Robert	LJB
Walker, Richard	Berry	65	04 Nov 1682	Newtowne		PH
Wheatley, Andrew	Nintoquint	116	13 Mar 1684	Newtowne		PH
Wheatley, Andrew	Wheatley's Hills	28	13 Mar 1684	Newtowne		PH, LJB
Wheatley, John	Wheatley's Meadows/ Batchelor's Comfort	110 190	01 Jan 1682	Newtowne	Norris, John	PH
Wood, William	Green Hill	250	01 Jan 1662	Newtowne	Ryley, John	PH, LJB

Ten Most Likely (names in bold print)

Abell, John	Beaverdam Manor / Saturday's Conclusion	300	1 Jan 1697	Resurrect		
Bayley/Bailey, John	Bayley's Rest / Small Hope	350	24 Aug 1694	Newtowne	Tenant: Waters, Joseph	
Bell, Daniel	Hopewell	200	06 May 1686	Poplar Hill		
Bennett, Richard	Bennett/Tunnel	200	01 Jan 1651	Poplar Hill		
Campbell, John	Oyster Shell Neck	50	01 Jan 1666	Poplar Hill		
Clark, Robert	St. Lawrence Freehold	100	01 Jan 1652	Newtowne		

Drury, Robert	Dry Dockin Addition	100	20 Oct 1683	Newtowne	Tant, James
Fosse, John	Shocke Park	100	15 Feb 1683	Newtowne	
Gough, James	*St. Margaret's*	300	Tenant / Possessor	Newtowne	Owner: (dec) Walter Pake
Hammond, John (Jr.)	*Lewgar's Plains*	430	01 Jul 1682	Newtowne	Tenant: Norris, John
Heard/Hurd, John (Jr.)	Heard's Choice Coventry / Offley	150 100 180	22 Oct 1681	Newtowne	Widow Susanna Heard
Jarbo, Henry	St. Anne / Peter's Hill St. Francis	100 500	Tenant / Possessor	Newtowne	Owner: (dec) Walter Pake
Norris, John	*Lewgar's Plains* Wheatley's Meadows	430 110	Tenant / Possessor	Newtowne	Owner: John Hammond
Ryley/Riley, John	Green Hill	250	Tenant / Possessor	Newtowne	Owner: William Wood
Tant/Taunt, James	Dry Dockin Addition	100	Tenant / Possessor	Newtowne	Owner: Robert Drury
Taylor, Henry	Kingstown	50		Newtowne	John Fosse
Thompson, Arthur	**Hownestow St. Oswald/ Hampstead**	100 400		Poplar Hill Newtowne	William Farthing John Bayley
Wheatley, John	**Wheatley's Meadows Batchelor's Comfort**	110 190		Newtowne	John Norris John Tant
Wood, William	Green Hill	250		Newtowne	John Ryley

Here are some of the stories of the men who might have been involved in the burning of Moll's hut. John Abell is the first name to consider. John was born in 1679 and died in 1746. His parents were Samuel Abell and Anne, and his paternal grandfather was Captain Robert Abell. John's first wife is unidentified, but his second wife was Frances Hutchins. Frances and John had sons Enoch and Cuthbert. This family owned land named "Beaverdam Manor" and "Saturday's Conclusion" in Resurrection Hundred, which was located adjacent to Newtowne Hundred. The Abell name is included in this list because it was found within most of the family genealogies that were investigated in St. Mary's County. Although he resided in Resurrection Hundred, he had connections to many of the other names on this list and was considered a man of influence and power in the county. Abell is still a prominent name there today.

Richard Bennett, who was born in 1644, was known to own parcels called "Bennett" and "Tunnel," a total of two hundred acres in the Poplar Hill Hundred very close to Moll Dyer's residence. It is not known exactly when he died, but his widow, Sarah Bennett, married John Taylor, and the Bennetts had children Richard, Sarah and others. Taylor was known to be an "Ordinary Keeper" on the Bennett land, and most likely the land and the trade was passed on to the Bennett heirs.[18]

According to an article by Philip H. Love,[19] Woodrow Bennett (born circa 1915) was the owner of a store in the area of Moll Dyer Run and knew that he was a descendant of the Bennetts involved in the burning of Moll Dyer's hut. He was quoted in the article as saying, "The Bennetts were one of the families she put her curse on." According to Nancy Glenn, resident of Moll Dyer Road from 1970 to 1975 and regular patron of the Bennett Store, Woodrow firmly believed that his family suffered as a result of the curse of Moll Dyer. He refused to discuss it further. Bennett said that his son had been killed at a young age in Germany, and his grandson had been killed in an auto accident.

Woodrow Bennett was listed as a resident of Leonardtown until 1996. Further investigation has revealed more details about Woodrow Wilson Bennett and his family. The earliest record of him is the 1930 Census, when he was living with his brother Rollins Bennett. No male was listed old enough to be his father, but a woman fifty years old was listed and assumed to be his mother, Blanche I. Bennett. There were four other males in the household, all close to Woodrow in age, and assumed to be brothers Thomas Bennett (twenty-eight), Henry Bennett (twenty-five), Richard Bennett (ten) and John Bennett (eight). The girls in the household were assumed to be Woodrow's sisters, M. Elizabeth Bennett (sixteen) and Virginia Bennett (thirteen).[20] Woodrow was born on November 6, 1912, in Leonardtown, Maryland, and in 1940 he was six feet tall, 145 pounds and had blue eyes and brown hair with a ruddy complexion. He lived on his own in Hollywood, Maryland, and was a single farmer.[21] The 1940 U.S. Census reveals more information about him. By the time the census was taken, he had married Dorothy Wise and had a son Woodrow Bennett, age three, and daughter Dorothy Bennett, age two. He was renting his house/farm in rural St. Mary's County, Maryland, and reported that he had completed seventh grade.[22]

The Bennetts had a total of four sons: Woodrow Wilson Bennett Jr. (born in 1937), Richard Henry Bennett (1941), Franklin Winfield Bennett (1943) and Robert Jennings Bennett (1955). There were two daughters listed: Dorothy Elizabeth Bennett (born 1937) and a second daughter, unnamed. No grandchildren were listed who would have died before Woodrow was last listed in 1996. Records show that the death of Woodrow Wilson Bennett Jr. tragically occurred on December 28, 1970, in Germany.[23] It was confusing to see that both Woodrow and Dorothy were born in 1937; an examination of the Social Security Death Records revealed each of the birthdays and clarified the question. His birthday was January 17, 1937, and hers was December 20, 1937—a busy year for their parents.[24]

No death information for Woodrow Bennett was found, but Dorothy Wise Bennett, born on May 2, 1917, died on November 14, 1997, with her last residence Leonardtown, St. Mary's County, Maryland.[25] Whether or not the death of Woodrow Wilson Bennett Jr. at age thirty-three constitutes proof of the existence of Moll Dyer's curse is irrelevant. It was a tragedy for Woodrow and Dorothy and considered a curse by Woodrow. One other Bennett connection to the Moll Dyer era is that one of the women tried for witchcraft in Maryland was named Elizabeth Bennett. See chapter 3 about other witches in Maryland for her complete story, but it is interesting to see that same name in modern times in the same area and connected to the Moll Dyer legend.

Robert Clark Jr. was born in 1650 and died in 1726. He was married twice, first to Sarah Combs and then to Elizabeth. He was a planter and held the office of appraiser in 1676, 1696, 1698 and 1701. His children were Thomas, Robert, Benjamin, Sarah Grinnell, Anne Hall, Jeny Gough and Elinor Grinnell (wife of Henry). His landholdings included "St. Lawrence Freehold," one hundred acres in Newtowne Hundred and a parcel located in Resurrection Hundred.[26] He is considered on this list because of his age, forty-seven, in 1697, and because he was a man of influence and position at the time. He would have had a vested interest in eliminating the witch's curse.

James Gough's birth date is not known, but his will is dated December 18, 1725, and was probated on January 31, 1725 (1726). In that will, he listed his wife, Elizabeth, and children James, Stephen, Peter, Baptista, Elizabeth and Ann. He also willed the three-hundred-acre land parcel called "St. Margaret's," to be divided up between son and brother, with two hundred acres going to James and one hundred acres to be sold to his brother Benjamin.[27] The most interesting thing about Gough is that he owned the land closest to where Moll Dyer Road is now located. He would have definitely been aware of the efforts to rid the area of Moll Dyer since he would have been one of the closest neighbors and most likely affected by her presence. He and his brother Benjamin would have very likely participated in the burning of her hut.[28] This parcel of land can be traced to the current residents of Moll Dyer Road.

John Hammond is on this list because he was listed as the owner of "Lewgar's Plains," 430 acres in Newtowne, the parcel second closest to the location of Moll Dyer's hut. No information tying him to the event has been found, but he would have definitely been a stakeholder in the effort to remove her from the land that was so close to his.

Henry Jarbo was born in 1673 and died 1708. By the time he died, he had owned one thousand acres in Newtowne Hundred. The parcels were named "St. Peter's Hill," "St. Lawrence," "St. John's" and "Marshes Hope."[29] He had apparently sold off everything except "St. Peter's Hill," because he only mentioned the five hundred acres of that parcel in his will.[30] Jarbo owned so much land in the area where Moll Dyer lived, he would have been very

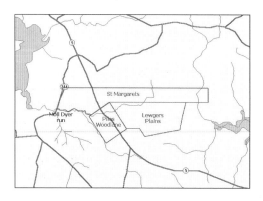

Diagram of "St. Margaret's" and "Lewgar's Plains"—land parcels where Moll Dyer's hut was likely located. *St. Mary's County Historical Society, Peter Himmelheber.*

interested in ridding the community of the witch. Just twenty-five years old and in the prime of his life, he would have had the energy and enthusiasm to be a part of the crowd.

John Norris Jr., who was born about 1681 and died in 1748, was the tenant/possessor of two parcels of land, "Lewgar's Plains" (430 acres) and "Wheatley's Meadows" (110 acres). Lewgar's Plains was owned by John Hammond, who was mentioned previously. John Norris was only sixteen years old when Moll Dyer was burned out of her hut, so he may not have been occupying the land at that time. However, he might have participated in such a crowd. Lewgar's Plains was close to the area where Moll lived, so he is included in this list of the ten most likely to have been involved. He married a woman named Ann, and they went on to have nine children between 1728 and 1748, when John died. Their children were Thomas (1728), John (1729), Susanna (1732), William (1734), Matthew (1737), Monica (1740), Clement (1742), Stephen (1744) and John Baptista (1748). John's father was John Norris, who died in 1710, and his mother was named Susanah.[31]

Henry Taylor owned a parcel called "Kingstown," which was fifty acres in Newtowne near the Moll Dyer residence. It is not known when he was born, but he died in 1719, which made him of an age to have participated in the hut burning. He also had a tenant/possessor living on the parcel named John Fosse, who was born in 1639 and died in 1713, making him of age to have also been a participant. The location of this parcel makes these two men likely candidates. Fosse/Fossee proved to be an interesting character. He was listed as a planter, probably a widower, Roman Catholic and a householder. There were two daughters, Treacha Fossee and Ruth Thomas. Ruth was married to Herbert Thomas. Land parcels listed for John Fossee in 1705 were "Shocke Park," "Hampton," "Kingston/Kingstown" and "Nunns Oak." They were all located in Newtowne Hundred and totaled two hundred acres. The Hampton parcel connected John Fossee/Fossey/Fosse with John Wheatley and Henry Taylor. The most interesting fact, however, was that he was the defendant in an action brought against him by William Herbert for using force to evict Herbert from his leased premises and "did other harm to William Herbert." The judgment was for the plaintiff in this case, and Fossee was fined fifty pounds sterling.[32] The incident documented here at least demonstrates that Fosse was capable of violence and most probably would have been involved in the Moll Dyer event.

The next name on this list is an eleventh great-uncle of the author, Arthur Thompson. According to family research, he was born in 1628 in England and arrived in Maryland in 1660 (indentured) and was free in 1670 in time to purchase a land parcel of one hundred acres named "Hownestow" in 1673; by 1683, he owned five hundred acres in Newtowne Hundred. They were named "Hownestow," "St. Oswald" and "Hampstead." Thompson was a carpenter by trade, Roman Catholic and married to Susan Carberry, most likely his second wife. He also owned three hundred acres called "Finchley" in St. Clements Hundred and one thousand acres called "Thompson's Choice" in Baltimore County. He and Susan had seven children: Mildred, Oswald, Sebastian, John, Jaclee, Margaret and Tecla.

Arthur Thompson was the subject of many legal actions during his life in St. Mary's County, from defaulting on a debt and trespassing in 1676 to being the defendant in a disturbing the peace action in which he, along with Thomas Gerard and Robert Stye, was "accused of assembling themselves together and with swords, staves and knives enter[ing] the house of Robert Browne, threatening to eject him." In 1684, the grand jury failed to reach a decision in this case, but there is reason to believe that Thompson could have been involved in a violent action such as burning Moll's hut. He fled the county to avoid the payment of another fine of 1,700 pounds of tobacco, plus additional fines of 283 and 415 pounds of tobacco in 1702. Shortly thereafter, Thompson died, leaving Susan his widow, but he left many descendants as a definite legacy in St. Mary's County.[33]

The last name on the list is John Wheatley, who owned 300 acres in two parcels named "Wheatley's Meadows" (110) and "Batchelor's Comfort" (190) in Newtowne. His birth date is unknown, but he died in 1717 and had a tenant/possessor on this land named John Norris, discussed earlier. He was married to Elizabeth and had children James, John, Joseph, Thomas, Francis, Winifred, Ann, Elizabeth, Susannah and Mary. Given the location of these parcels, the tenant who was a likely participant and having several sons of the age to be involved, Wheatley is considered a possible candidate in this search.[34]

From this list of "persons of interest" emerge the names that have produced descendants who reside in St. Mary's County today. It is likely these descendants have been some of the perpetuators of the legend of Moll Dyer. Efforts have been made to interview some of them to see if they believe the curse is still in effect. Those results are found in part III, "The Curse Continues, or Does It?"

Two more questions remain to be answered about those who lived in that area. Who represented the law at that time, and would he have been involved in this at all? From the historical records for that period, there seemed to be no one who was actually in charge. John Coode Sr., who was listed as the county sheriff from 1694 to 1696, was busy with four other men and seven hundred followers trying to overthrow Maryland's government from 1689 on. The next sheriff listed is Henry Lowe, from 1698 to 1700, so the year 1697 seemed to fall through the legal crack as far as law enforcement for St. Mary's County was concerned.[35] No one was in charge. The records seem to indicate that the citizens were responsible for themselves.

This list of men and tenants/possessors constitutes the men who were most likely involved in burning Moll Dyer's hut that cold winter's night. It certainly does not mean that they were all definitely involved, just possible participants. The curse that was attributed to Moll as she froze to death was a result of the mass guilt that these neighbors of hers must have felt when they learned of the unintended end of the witch they so much wanted out of their lives. That guilt compelled these families, as well as other neighbors not directly involved, to tell and retell the story over the years in an effort to keep alive the story of unintentional tragedy. If they had blamed her for their misfortunes and illnesses, then they must have believed that she had the power to curse them for what they had done. The winter weather probably continued to be severe and illness rampant, which fueled the belief that they had been cursed. After all, ridding themselves of the witch didn't change their circumstances or make things better.

After considering all these possible participants in the mob responsible for Moll's tragic end, the last question was to consider the name "Dyer." Were there any possible relatives of Mary Dyer residing locally who could have helped in her hour of need? No landowners by that name were found in St. Mary's County at all in the last half of the seventeenth century. There was a record of an indentured servant by the name of John Dyer who apparently was the servant of John Elly in 1671–72. He was named in Elly's will and bequeathed a "yearling calf."[36] After that date, there were men by the name of John Dyer found living in Baltimore in the Quaker Church records and one found who lived in Dorchester County and died there in 1727. His will was dated December 22, 1727, and probated on June 5, 1728. In it, his occupation was given as a planter, and his heirs were listed as Martha, his wife; Thomas William, his son; Katherine, his son's wife; and their sons, Thomas and James, John's grandsons.[37] It was likely that John Dyer, John Elly's indentured servant, was released from his indenture after Elly's death and moved across the Chesapeake to Dorchester County to live out his life. There were not many Quakers who came to Maryland as indentured servants, so that removed the John Dyer of Baltimore from consideration. Mary Dyer's closest relative would have been her brother William in Prince George's County, too far away to have helped her.

How could these simple people have supported the legal prosecution of witchcraft, let alone taken the law into their own hands to rid themselves of the problem? Ignorance of weather phenomena and what caused it was understandable. It was a sophisticated concept and is still studied at length today by educated scientists of meteorology. Knowledge of medicine was basically nonexistent, and an epidemic of influenza was a devastating and horrifying threat to their very existence in a hostile environment. However, it was ironic that Moll fell victim to the hysteria of people who professed to share tolerance for "other" religious beliefs. To simply state it, meteorology and medicine were sciences that were considered religious ideas at that time. The witches of the seventeenth century were the scientists of the eighteenth century, and their remedies are still used today under the umbrella of holistic medicine.

Part Three

THE CURSE CONTINUES...
OR DOES IT?

Moll Dyer Saga Continues

The famous legend of the witch Moll Dyer of St. Mary's County, Maryland, is not the end of the supernatural intrigue that has continued to this day in the area known as Moll Dyer Road and Moll Dyer Run, where Moll lived and died. With Moll's story as a prologue, this is another bizarre story of a seemingly cursed woman, also named Mary, who was doomed to join Moll as a restless spirit roaming the same terrain.

In 1940, a mixed-race couple lived in that area back in the woods away from public view and the prejudice they faced at that time. His name was John Thomas Hatfield, a divorced white man, and hers was Mary Bell Thompson, a black woman and widow. The U.S. Census reported them living in Leonardtown on Glebe Road in 1940.[38] Who were they, and how did they end up in the town of Leonardtown? They were both from elsewhere and knew hardly anyone. What strange sequence of events happened to include them in the legend of Moll Dyer? Why is she called the "Black Moll Dyer"? The answers to those questions lie in the journey that each of them traveled to bring them together in St. Mary's in 1940.

John Thomas Hatfield Jr. was born on April 5, 1883, in Lee County, South Carolina. His father was John Thomas Hatfield Sr., and he died in 1939. His mother was Martha Cornelia "Mattie" Shiver, who died in 1929. His parents married in 1873 in Sumter County. John Jr. died on December 29, 1969,[39] back in Sumter, South Carolina.[40] The story of this family took place in Sumter County, South Carolina, it would seem. That was the beginning and end of his story, but the sojourn to St. Mary's County, Maryland, would prove the most unusual episode of his life.

Fourteen years after John was born, Mary B. Thompson was born in October 1897 in South Carolina, the daughter of Rolt (Robert) and Pender Thompson, both age thirty-three in 1900. This black family were also residents of Sumter County, South Carolina, and had five children, Mary being the youngest.[41] At this point in time, there was no apparent connection between John and Mary Bell or their families.

In 1910, in Sumter County, John Thomas Hatfield was married to spouse Ida, age twenty-six, and they had three children.[42] That same year, Mary B. Thompson was eleven and still living in the household of her father, Robert Thompson, but her mother, Pender, was no longer with them. The family was still residing in Sumter County. In the household with her were two sisters and one older brother.[43] Still, there seemed to be simply a parallel between their lives, with no known intersection.

By 1920, Ida Irene Hatfield was a single head of household in Sumter, South Carolina, with five children living with her, aged five to sixteen. John Thomas Hatfield was not mentioned as being there.[44] They appeared to have been divorced. That year's census reveals that Mary Thompson was twenty-two, race mulatto, single and born in South Carolina. She could read and write, and she resided as a boarder with the family of Joseph Brown (black), including his wife and five children, in Saint George, Dorchester County, South Carolina.[45]

In 1930, John Thomas Hatfield, age forty-seven, was again reportedly married, but to his second wife, Mary, age fifty-five, living in Sumter County, South Carolina, with their five-year-old son. Both adults had been twenty years of age when first married, but not to each other. It seems that John divorced Ida, met and married Mary and had a five-year-old son in the ten years since he disappeared from his first household.[46] That same year, Mary Bell (Thompson) Jacobs, age thirty, was the wife of Sam Jacobs, age forty-eight, and mother of A.J. Jacobs, age eight. They had probably married around 1921 to have an eight-year-old child. They were residents of Hoke County, North Carolina.[47] In April 1931, Mary Bell's husband, Sam, passed away in North Carolina, leaving her a widow with a nine-year-old son.[48] At this point Mary probably returned to her home in Sumter County to support herself and her son with the help of her older siblings and father. It is very likely that she found employment as a domestic for a white family because that is one of the few options open to a young black woman to earn a living in South Carolina in 1931.

In 1940, Ida Hatfield was again listed as married with John living in the household in Sumter, South Carolina, along with child Irene, age seven.

Ida was a nurse with an eighth-grade education; John was reported to have a fifth-grade education.[49] The story is puzzling during this period because John was listed as married to Mary in 1930 but back with Ida in 1940 after fathering another child with her in 1933. Had he left second wife, Mary, and returned to remarry Ida? This was his first wife, but where was John really? Actually, he was not in South Carolina at all, but found to be a resident of Maryland. No record has been found to determine what happened to Mary Hatfield after her marriage to John, as listed in the 1930 census record. She could have divorced John and married someone else or died, leaving him to return to Ida.

The most compelling development for John and Mary Bell is that they met and fell in love before 1940. She very likely had taken a job as a maid for John and Mary or John and Ida, whomever he happened to be living with. They became involved and decided to flee the social shunning they would face in their hometown and Sumter County. Mixed-race couples were not tolerated in South Carolina in the 1930s. They fled to the more tolerant area in Maryland, to a secluded house in the dense woods among predominantly black neighbors at that time.

The 1940 Census recorded a forty-one-year-old black woman named Marybelle Thompson, born in 1898 in Maryland, living as a servant in the household of John Thomas Hatfield, age fifty-seven, divorced and born in Washington, D.C. The residence was on Glebe Road in St. Mary's County, Maryland, which is now called Fairgrounds Road.[50] They appeared to have left their respective homes and relocated there. She had dropped her married name of Jacobs, and neither claimed South Carolina as a birthplace, but they were definitely the couple residing in the woods at the end of Moll Dyer Road. Maybe they did that to attempt some anonymity in an era of racial discrimination and prejudice.

The 1942 military draft record (World War II) for John Thomas Hatfield, born in 1883 in Lee County, South Carolina, whose mother was Mattie and father J.T. Hatfield, revealed that he was living in St. Mary's County, Maryland, and listed the permanent contact for him as William Wise of Leonardtown, Maryland, probably a war buddy from World War I.[51]

This trail of census information brought John and Mary Bell together and living in Leonardtown. How they arrived there was a mystery, but one possibility was that they met in South Carolina, fell in love and escaped to St. Mary's County, Maryland, to be together without being known by anyone in the area except for John's friend, William Wise. John left two wives and eight children to be with Mary, and she left her son, probably with her family, to be with him after her husband died.

Those are the facts that describe the couple known as John Hatfield and Mary Bell Thompson, who lived together in a house in the woods at the end of Moll Dyer Road. The area was also accessible from Beem Lane, a road that went south from Fairgrounds Road (known as Glebe Road at that time)—hence the reference to Glebe Road on the census document. The most direct route to their location was Moll Dyer Road, and that is where they lived together in the woods hidden from public scrutiny. Many of the other residents of Moll Dyer Road at that time were black families, who would have been more tolerant of the couple than white neighbors. Of course, the legendary witch of St. Mary's County also resided and died in that same area 250 years earlier.

Land records of St. Mary's County contain a deed for fifty acres of land purchased from Enoch A. Norris by J.T. "Slim" Hatfield dated May 17, 1938. The parcel of land was known as "St. Margaret's."[52] Later in the same year, on June 25, John Thomas Hatfield sold eight acres of this land to Mary Bell Jacobs Thompson[53] that was presumed to be the location of the house that he built for her. This land parcel is also located where Moll Dyer's hut probably was sited and referenced in the chapter that covers the citizens of the county who would have been involved in burning Moll's hut.

John and Mary lived as husband and wife and wanted to spend eternity together there in their wooded home. John built two tombs for their eternal rest in the woods behind their house. Little did they expect that they would be needed very quickly. Mary died on July 10, 1942, and was laid to rest in one of the tombs in the woods.

A copy of the death certificate for Mary Bell Thompson Jacobs revealed that she died of chronic kidney disease. The name of the informant was listed as George Jacobs, her son, and her husband was listed as Washington Jacobs.[54] Actually, George Jacobs was her nephew, and Washington Jacobs was George's father and Mary's brother-in-law, brother of her deceased husband, Sam L. Jacobs.[55] Maybe it was just easier to claim to be her son when asked to give the information to the doctor or undertaker at the time. Nevertheless, this added an element of doubt to that document.

On September 13, 1942, John Thomas "Slim" Hatfield sold the fifty acres known as "St. Margaret's" to T. Foley Drury with the exception of the burial ground for Mary Bell Jacobs Thompson (deceased) and John Thomas Hatfield.[56] The eight acres that Hatfield had deeded to Mary Bell had reverted to his ownership by the terms of her will.

Headstone of Mary Bell Thompson with inscription shown on her tomb. *Photo by the author.*

Much of the rest of the story is based on folklore known and related by residents of the area for the last seventy years. Nancy Glenn was a local resident who lived in the area during the 1970s and claimed that Mary Bell Thompson and John Hatfield lived together in a small house that had a stairway in the middle and a kumquat tree outside. She reported Mary Bell to be a tiny person who supposedly died during childbirth. That fact has not been verified, and no reference to any baby has been found. Kidney disease was listed as the cause of her death.

Peter Himmelheber, St. Mary's County Historical Society member and local historian, reported that the story goes that John Hatfield was so overcome with grief at the loss of Mary Bell that he continually removed her corpse from the tomb and brought her into the house to be with him. After the situation was discovered, John was supposedly sent to Crownsville State Mental Hospital, Maryland, where he remained until his death in December 1969 and where he was also buried. Privacy laws in Maryland are very stringent and prohibit access to mental health records by anyone other than family. These bizarre circumstances and stories about him have not been substantiated, and it is certain that he died and was buried in South Carolina. Whether or not he was discovered practicing necrophilia with Mary Bell's corpse has not been determined, but it is one more bizarre twist to the story. It is true that he left the area shortly after her death.

On May 16, 2015, in an interview with Bernard Goldsborough of Lexington Park, Maryland, he recalled John Hatfield and Mary Bell Thompson lived on land that he had purchased from Lem Norris. According to his memories, Hatfield was a skilled carpenter and had rebuilt the dilapidated farmhouse on the land for the two of them to occupy. Goldsborough also remembered that John called her "Bell" and that she was an excellent cook. Hatfield and Bernard's father worked together and helped to build a garage at the St. Mary's Academy campus in Leonardtown and to build various structures on the property of Cuthbert Fenwick. These were the aspects of normalcy in the story of Mary Bell and John.

Goldsborough went on to relate that Hatfield seemed somewhat peculiar in many ways and suddenly went away after the death of Mary Bell for what seemed like a couple of years. This would mean that Hatfield returned in 1944. Goldsborough did not know for sure where Hatfield had gone, but when he returned to Leonardtown, he had a woman with him who would not live in the house that he had occupied with Mary Bell. Mr. Hatfield and this woman, who could have been one of his former wives or a sister, rented a house in the Hanover area from Cuthbert Fenwick while the original house was sold. After residing there for maybe two years, the two of them left the area and probably returned to South Carolina.

Actually, John Thomas Hatfield did return to Sumter County, South Carolina, sometime after 1942 and before he died in 1969.[57] At this point, nothing certain is known about his whereabouts between 1942 and 1969.

In November 1964, the *Enterprise*, a local newspaper, reported a grave-robbing crime by three local teenage boys. They broke into the tomb of Mary Bell Thompson, removed her skull from the remains and paraded through Leonardtown with the stolen cranium.[58] They were arrested and prosecuted for their crime, and Mary's skull was supposedly returned to her tomb and sealed up. If that were the case then, that is not how the story ended, as if it weren't enough to degrade Mary Bell with the macabre parade through the streets of Leonardtown.

The following Halloween, 1965, residents reported that the tomb was opened again by local teenage boys, but the skull was still there. They did not remove anything, but the tomb was left open, according to a local source who was involved and requested to remain anonymous. From that time on, the tomb was open, according to all who have seen it and been interviewed. Thus the tomb and the remains were left to the ravages of the elements, wildlife and local teenage population. Was the restless spirit of Moll Dyer at work here?

Gale Jones purchased the property in 1979 and has lived there since that time. He reported that the tomb has remained open the entire time he has lived there and that the skull has never been there. Currently, it remains open and a few of Mary Bell Thompson's bones are visible, but most of her remains are missing, including her skull. Whether the remains were stolen by persons roaming the woods or removed by animals, the resulting conclusion is that Mary Bell Thompson's spirit is not resting in peace, at the very least, and is most likely haunting the area along with the other restless spirit in the area, Moll Dyer.

Since the spirit of Mary Bell Thompson is present in the area already haunted by the spirit of Moll Dyer, she is referred to as the "Black Moll Dyer." Both are tormented spirits and have reasons to be restless and searching for peace or revenge. Although Mary Bell has never been accused of witchcraft, the strange and unsettling series of events after the end of

Mary Bell Thompson tomb (*left*) and John Hatfield tomb (*right*) showing the opening in hers. *Photo by the author.*

Close-up of the hole in Mary Bell Thompson's tomb. *Photo by the author.*

her life add her spirit to the eerie atmosphere of the area and the intrigue of the legend. Maybe Moll welcomed the company of Mary Bell and the added mystery to her own story. Thus the supernatural mystique for this area continues, and there are many who make Halloween pilgrimages each year to visit the haunting of the two Moll Dyers and the open tomb of Mary Bell Thompson. These two very restless kindred spirits, both named Mary, are bound to join them and anyone else who dares to visit the creepy Moll Dyer Run area of Leonardtown, a most intriguing and unnerving vicinity. It is anything but lonely.

8

Moll and the Weather

A Trip to the Woods

During the fall of 1984, Karen Stauffer and three high school girlfriends were out driving around one Saturday afternoon, looking for something to do in Leonardtown, Maryland. They happened to pass Moll Dyer Road traveling south on Maryland Route 5, Point Lookout Road. Karen felt the urge to turn left onto the road and drove along the narrow, wooded terrain late that afternoon. The fall colors were slowly drifting with the still air to the dry, leaf-blanketed ground. She had read an article about the possible discovery of the burned-out ruin of Moll Dyer's hut back in the legendary woods.

Karen felt compelled to go find the site to see where the legendary witch had once lived. The other girls didn't share her interest in doing that and expressed their preference to head to the mall and do some shopping. Karen insisted that they should take a walk and see if they could find the reported location of the hut. She said she felt something "not ordinary" pulling her to go there.

The weather was bright and sunny and calm with no threatening weather of any type when they pulled off the road and parked the car at the edge of the woods near the creek known as Moll Dyer Run. The three girls gave in about the mall trip, and all four got out of the car. They started off into the woods heading toward where the cabin foundation was reported to be found. It was quiet and calm as they walked, and there was no sound of animals or birds. That seemed unusual to them for a beautiful fall afternoon, but they kept on.

As they stomped through the leaves, vines and branches, the dense tree growth made the walk somewhat of a challenge, but they ventured on into the woods. As they approached the reported location of the hut ruins, the sky became overcast and the wind started to blow. The farther they went, the worse the weather became, until the wind became very strong and the temperature began to drop. The three girls with Karen wanted to turn around, but Karen insisted that they keep on to find the hut. She sensed a presence that urged her to keep on going.

When lightning struck close by and thunder rumbled immediately after, the four girls turned and ran back through the woods toward the car, with Karen in the rear. She recalled feeling as if someone was pursuing her and about to touch her as she ran away. She could hear the crunching of footsteps breaking twigs behind her as she fled in desperation to get away from whatever was happening. As they ran through the woods toward the car, the weather gradually subsided. By that time, the sun was shining again and the wind was quiet. It was as if nothing had just happened with the weather in the area. They were all completely spooked by the sequence of events, and Karen was obviously shaken up by what she had experienced.

They jumped back into the car, started the engine, turned around and drove away down Moll Dyer Road back to Point Lookout Road. The mall sounded like a much better option at that point. They were convinced that the curse of Moll Dyer had come into play as they came closer and closer to the site of Moll Dyer's legendary home. The legend about her command of the weather and the curse on that area definitely made a lasting impression on Karen and her friends. None of them ever ventured into that area again, convinced that they had experienced the presence of Moll herself that day.

Moll Taps the Weather Channel

In December 2013, the Weather Channel (TWC) was planning a new series called *Supernatural*. The producers wanted the first program to be about the legend of Moll Dyer and St. Mary's County. The series was classified a documentary about weather-related supernatural events, which by definition are based on factual occurrences. Since the production company was based in Baltimore, the producers were familiar with the legend of Moll Dyer. They knew the circumstances around her freezing to death during the weather event of the coldest night of the winter. It was to be the premiere episode in the series because the story was compelling and because the venue was close for them, especially for travel during the winter months.

The producers contacted the St. Mary's County Historical Society and requested interviews with all the local historians who had information and could contribute to their program. They wanted anyone who knew the particulars of the legend and facts surrounding it or who had experienced strange events in the area of Moll Dyer Road and Run. They signed up several participants and scheduled the filming for one week during the month of February 2014.

The schedule was set up, and each participant was assigned to be interviewed in various locations, with most of the sessions to be done at Tudor Hall, the headquarters of the historical society in Leonardtown. The parlor of Tudor Hall was staged with the cameras, dark drapes, candles and low lighting. There were separate sessions conducted in various locations covering the legend, the weather-related facts, the research regarding Moll's true identity, an encounter with the rock and several about personal experiences in the Moll Dyer Road area. There was filming outside in the setting sun (and cold) that went on until there was no light. As the sun set that evening, it was obvious that the program would include everything known at that time and be presented in a dramatic fashion.

On Friday afternoon, the Weather Channel crew was across the street from Tudor Hall at the county courthouse, filming right next to Moll Dyer's Rock. Elements of the curse associated with Moll Dyer and the rock are strange and extreme weather events, as well as injuries, illness and camera malfunctions.

What occurred then definitely involved the weather. The sky threatened rain as the clouds moved rapidly inland and a darkness fell over the small town center. As the rain, driven by the increasing wind, began to pelt the windows, the people at Tudor Hall received word that there was a tornado warning for Leonardtown, as one had been spotted nearby in Breton Bay heading for Leonardtown High School. Everyone was to go to the basement immediately. They waited in the stone basement of the old house while the wind howled outside and drove the raindrops to tap out their rhythm against the thick wavy glass windowpanes. As the intensity of the storm subsided, the nervous patrons received notice that it was all clear to return to the library on the second floor. A glance out the windows

Tudor Hall, home of the St. Mary's County Historical Society (circa 1750). *Photo by the author.*

didn't indicate that the tornado had come close; however, that didn't mean that there had not been one.

Back in the library, one of the ladies was on her cellphone and received word that there had been a tornado that had come across Leonardtown High School, the county fairgrounds, Fairgrounds Road and Romanus Drive. Although it did not directly strike there in downtown Leonardtown, the area where it did travel was only about four miles away, not far for a weather event like a tornado. The path that the tornado took was within a mile of the Moll Dyer Run area. Damage included many downed trees along Fairgrounds Road and approximately twenty-five trees on two residences along Romanus Drive, with twenty in the author's front yard alone. This event was connected to TWC production, Moll Dyer's location and the author—quite a coincidence.

Tornadoes are rare in Southern Maryland, and to have one in the month of February is simply unheard of. This was a highly unusual weather phenomenon recorded that day. Could it possibly have been an effort by Moll Dyer to exhibit her power and be recognized by TWC producers? It was intriguing to think that Moll had made an appearance to impress the filmmakers in Leonardtown. However, the producers did not take note of the tornado or include any mention of it in the program.

Her efforts ignored, Moll apparently went further to impress them. Several days after filming was completed, a request came from the producer to ask if participants would consent to another session of filming. Why? The card in the camera failed. There was no explanation for the failure, at least that they provided—or was there? One of the effects of the curse surrounding the rock was that cameras would not work. Another session of filming at Tudor Hall was scheduled that basically covered the incident of touching the rock and left out the research into Moll's identity.

When the program finally aired, there was not a word about the work to identify the real woman who was Moll Dyer, Mary Dyer of Devon, England. The facts were not interesting enough for the program, or maybe Moll just wasn't ready then for the world to know who she really was when she affected the card in the camera.

Was this the curse at work in the present age? Was it mere coincidence? Possibly either or both? The answers to these questions remain in the eye of the beholder, just as the legend lives on from the perspective of those affected by such "coincidences." It is left for each reader to reach his own conclusion.

9

Residents' and Relatives' Curse Update

To evaluate the presence of Moll Dyer's curse today, the people most likely to be affected by it need to give their perspectives. Those cursed, according to the legend, were those who lived in the area where Moll died and the people who have descended from those who persecuted her. Here are some of those to consider.

The only evidence of anyone living in the Moll Dyer Road/Run area talking openly about being cursed by Moll Dyer was the story of Mr. Bennett in the 1970s and covered in depth in the "Whodunit" chapter. He lived about one mile away from the location of where the rock was found. He definitely believed that his family had been cursed because of the untimely death of his son and reportedly his grandson. No currently living relatives could be located to determine if that opinion continues. Records show that all three of the remaining sons were deceased by 2012. The only one who resided in St. Mary's County did not leave any children. The daughters all had moved out of the state. Possibly, the fact that no descendants exist in the county today could indicate that Bennett was right about the curse on his family—or could it possibly be a self-fulfilling prophesy, as a result of the general feeling of guilt?

Most of the residents of Moll Dyer Road since 1960 have reported that their long and normal lives in the area have been without any apparent curse. Edith McFadden, who grew up on the road and is now seventy-five years old, reported that she was told the story of Moll Dyer as a child as a deterrent to any misbehavior, the consequences being a visit from the local witch. She grew up with a healthy respect for the possibility of Moll's existence but did not recall any specific instances of dire consequences resulting because of her transgressions.

The Holly family, longtime residents of the road, chuckle when the subject of the legend is brought up and believed that the biggest curse related to the legend was the removal of the rock when the National Guard "tore up their yard." They didn't appreciate all the attention the event attracted or the heavy equipment used to extract it from the deep woods. They all have been content to live in a beautiful, quiet, peaceful, secluded and wooded area of the county and hope that Moll and her story don't cause any more excitement.

Nancy Glenn reported at first that she seemed "blessed by Moll Dyer" because her two sons were born while she lived on Moll Dyer Road from 1970 to 1975. Then, when she thought about it, she remembered that she had also suffered two miscarriages during that period, events that she considered a tragedy and possibly a curse at the time. She and her husband had visited the rock deep in the woods, and she had touched it. Was it just bad luck, or was it the curse of Moll Dyer? She continues to consider the possibility.

Although Nancy reported that she was not nervous about living in the area at that time, she did report a weather-related incident that could have been disastrous while she was living there. One fall day, her husband, Morris, was set to bring down a tree that needed to be removed before the winter weather started. He had set everything up to fell the tree in a particular direction, and the wind was calm so that the tree would fall where he wanted it. Nancy had their toddler son Lawson outside on the patio to watch his father at work. When Morris started the chainsaw and cut through the trunk of the tree, the wind suddenly picked up and caused the tree to fall in the wrong direction. It began to fall straight toward the patio where Lawson was playing. Nancy screamed for Lawson to run just as the tree crashed down across the patio where he had just been. So, did Moll cause the wind to suddenly change direction, or did she save the day by alerting Nancy of the impending doom? That day and the incident reminded her of the curse on the area where they once lived.

The Glenn sons who were born on Moll Dyer Road grew up roaming the area because they moved only about a mile away when they left the road. If anyone could have sensed the effects of the curse on the area, they are the perfect candidates. Two teenage boys, along with their neighborhood friends, knew every inch of the woods and everything going on there.

Lawson and Latham Glenn grew up in the area close to Moll Dyer Road and Run and spent many days and hours riding their bicycles on the gravel roads and trails surrounding the creek bed of Moll Dyer Run. The road was not much more than a single-lane dead-end road through the dense woods and provided a quiet bicycle trail, too. One afternoon in the fall of 1982 when they were ten and eight years old, they were riding together following the creek bed where the bank was exposed when it had not rained in a while. It was covered with gravel and moss but an area where leaves did not hamper the bikes. When they stopped to rest for a minute and get a drink from the creek, they heard what sounded like footsteps coming toward them crunching the dead dry leaves and sticks that covered the woods floor. Since they were a little nervous about trespassing, they jumped back on their bikes and took off in the other direction toward home as quickly as possible. The farther they rode, the more they heard the heavy footsteps following their rapid retreat. They raced away from the sounds, thinking they were in trouble, but no one appeared to confront them. Lawson remembers the feeling of terror that they never saw anyone who might have caused the sound of footsteps. He thinks to this day that Moll Dyer was trying to scare them away from doing any mischief in her woods since they were unpredictable children, and it had worked.

Latham is the younger of the two Glenn brothers and by far the more adventurous. He spent his adolescence roaming the woods along with several of his neighborhood friends. They knew everything that went on in the woods around Moll Dyer Road and Run during the late 1980s and early 1990s. He acknowledged that the Mary Bell Thompson open tomb was an epicenter of attraction for the local teen boys. He admitted to removing one of the bones from her open tomb, an example of the typical activities that attracted the boys to that location and indication of the disposition of her remains. Another one of his friends took the loose headstone from the tomb and threw it into a pond nearby. One of the boys "ratted" on him to his father, who made him go into the pond and retrieve it. It was returned and permanently reattached to the tomb. The scariest episode for the boys was when they were walking through the woods on the path to the tomb and encountered two people dressed all in black running out of the woods away from the tomb. They appeared scared, as if they had been interrupted doing something strange at the tomb site. The boys were extremely unnerved by that encounter, but it did not keep them away from the intriguing location where Moll and Mary's spirits roam.

They regarded the spooky events there to be a part of the ambiance of the general area, but they don't feel that any curse was at work to thwart their adventures in Moll's woods. They have a great respect for the legend and the atmosphere of intrigue in the area that they called home.

Gale Jones, resident of the road since 1979, experienced a little apprehension regarding Moll right after he moved in when the battery in his car was dead and he was trying to deal with it in the dark of night. He felt a little creepy when he had to navigate in the dark to recharge the battery, anticipating the possible presence of the legendary witch. Despite his uneasiness, he completed the chore without any incident. Other than that, he had no uneasiness over the years and seems very happy to inhabit the land where Moll most likely resided. Gale also owns the land where the Mary Bell Thompson open tomb is located and gives "ghost walks" out there at Halloween. He seems to be enjoying the legend and intrigue from the stories of Moll Dyer and Mary Bell Thompson. Has Moll Dyer been an advantage to Gale over the years? He definitely doesn't suffer at the hands of the local celebrity.

The land where Moll lived was supposedly cursed, too, and bound to be a barren area where crops wouldn't grow. At least, that is the way the story goes. A walk in the woods along Moll Dyer Road and Run will reveal that it is a rocky, hilly area, heavily wooded and difficult to walk through. There are several farms in the area today, however, and as far as can be determined, the crops have grown very well since the 1980s. Those that have chosen to farm the land seem to have been successful in that endeavor, growing corn, soybeans, wheat and other crops.

Fred Benton retired as job training and safety director for Southern Maryland Electric Cooperative (SMECO) in 1998 after working there for thirty-eight years. He was called to the local offices to respond to emergency alarms that frequently went off in the middle of severe weather incidents. Leonardtown's local office was often the site where he had to respond to such emergency alarms during the years of his career. He felt that the area surrounding Moll Dyer Road and the creek named Moll Dyer Run were very often parts of the area in which the weather events such as thunderstorms, snowstorms and floods appeared to be the worst.

Living in St. Mary's City, fifteen miles south of Leonardtown, he had to travel through that area to arrive at the Leonardtown office and any of the other offices that were in the northern part of the county. He often wondered about the area and the curse of Moll Dyer as he passed the road.

The intersection of Moll Dyer Road and Point Lookout Road (Maryland Route 5) is a place that is located at the bottom of a steep hill. The Moll Dyer Run meanders along the side of Moll Dyer Road and crosses Point Lookout Road just south of the entrance to Moll Dyer Road. There are steep ditches on either side of Point Lookout Road at that location, and there is a concrete culvert under Point Lookout Road where Moll Dyer Run crosses under it. It is a very hilly section of the road there. Usually there is no water in the ditches, and Moll Dyer Run trickles along and under Point Lookout Road.

In 1998, Fred remembered a particularly severe thunderstorm and rain event that triggered a safety alarm in Leonardtown. As he drove north on Point Lookout Road, the storm intensified more and more as he approached the vicinity of Moll Dyer Road. The rain came down so hard that he could hardly see to drive and stay on the road. The lightning flashed, and the thunder followed almost immediately. He could just envision the downed trees and power lines that SMECO was going to have to deal with when it was over. The storm was dumping an incredible volume of water in that area.

As he approached the Moll Dyer Road turnoff on the right, he was forced to pull off the road and stop suddenly when he realized that the Moll Dyer Run had flooded across Point Lookout Road and filled the deep ditches that lined the road. There was no place to go except the immediate shoulder of the road as the water was already about to cross the road. He sat in his car and waited for something to change, but it just seemed to get worse by the minute. This was a flash flood coming from Moll Dyer Run. Before he could turn around to try to find another route to Leonardtown, a pickup truck came floating down the flooded ditch on the side of the road. This was the worst flooding that he had ever witnessed since working for SMECO, and it was at the location that seemed to be the epicenter of bad weather over the years of his career. The Moll Dyer curse, relating particularly to the weather, did seem to be at work in the area where she had lived and died, at least to him. There was no doubt for him that she had actually existed.

Fred also knew the Farell family who lived on the property where the rock was reported to be located. Mr. Farell and his wife farmed the land adjacent to Moll Dyer Road with four sons. One of the sons, named Stanislos and called "Sandy," worked at SMECO with Fred and told the story of his father and brothers at the county fair. They woke up early the Saturday the fair was going on and went out to do their chores for the morning. When they were finished with the chores, the four brothers and their father walked a mile up the steep hill of Point Lookout Road to the fairgrounds.

The five of them arrived at the fair late in the morning, and each had worked up an appetite. They learned of a pancake-eating contest and decided to enter. As the contest progressed, the five Farells kept eating and ended up being the last ones standing to capture the title of champion. They came in first, second and third and captured the prize money, five, four and three dollars, respectively, but the contest ended only when the cooks ran out of pancake batter. The son who had come in first had devoured one hundred plate-sized pancakes—the two runners-up in the high nineties. All five had depleted the contest of the needed pancake ingredients and taken home the prize money.

Sandy told Fred that his father had told them on their walk back to the farm, "Don't tell your mother about the pancake-eating contest because she won't want to make us any supper!" Those residents of the hallowed ground where the infamous rock resided for most of their lives didn't seem cursed by Moll Dyer, except with bottomless pits for stomachs.

The name Thompson is very common in St. Mary's County, and most of the Thompsons who have been here for several generations are descendants of the original settlers and Arthur Thompson, one of the Ten Most Likely to have been involved with the burning of Moll's hut.

Kevin's Korner Kafe, just south of Leonardtown on Point Lookout Road, is an area significant to the Moll Dyer legend because of its proximity to the location where the local almshouse and pauper's burial field were located in 1697. That is where Moll was most likely buried. Kevin Thompson, the owner, is a Thompson descendant.

Kevin's story of his family and their immediate history contains no catastrophic events that he relates to any curse from Moll Dyer because of his lineage. Although his restaurant has only been in business in that location for a few years, the building has been there for more than thirty years. There must be some restless spirits in the neighborhood from that area, but he didn't suspect any supernatural activity, at least not yet.

He was not aware of the connection of his location to the particulars of the Moll Dyer story, but he certainly knows the Moll Dyer legend and the curse surrounding the area, the descendants and the rock. The one part of it that he believes is the negative energy associated with the rock. He chooses to be positive in his attitudes toward his family and his business and, consequently, has chosen to never go near the rock in Leonardtown and will not be doing so in the future. He believes that stone deserves a wide berth.

An unnamed resident, who lives in the area of Moll Dyer's hut site and curiously also is a Thompson relation, has revealed a surprising discovery in the heavily wooded area of his land. He has lived on his property for over thirty years and walked and explored the land all that time. A well-traveled path with a cluster of stones went unnoticed until the winter of 2018, when his curiosity about them was piqued. Since the vegetation had all died back and the stones were more visible than usual, he decided to do some digging and see what he could unearth.

Armed with a rake, a trowel and a camera to photograph whatever could be found, he went into the woods and out to the site. First, he raked the ground covered in leaves to see how many stones there actually were to be seen. There were a total of twelve within an eight-foot distance and configured in an *L* shape. He dug around the stones to see what lay below the surface and unearthed a broken brick, which he photographed and removed to take to the Archeology Department at St. Mary's College of Maryland in St. Mary's City. He figured that if it were a modern brick, then he could just give up the project.

The brick went to visit the college and received the evaluation of being "pre–Civil War" because it was handmade. Since all bricks before the Civil War were handmade, it was impossible to definitely date it without more artifacts that might be buried at the site, such as glass or pottery or tools. That was all he needed to hear. He was off to uncover more. He was told to dig carefully, using a brush to clean away debris, and to use a metal probe to find other large stones under the surface.

Back to the site with a wagon full of tools, a tape measure and a camera, he continued to unearth large stones in a straight line from the corner of the *L* for almost ten more feet before they turned in a perpendicular corner to the original corner about eighteen feet away. Careful excavation revealed small glass shards, all hand blown and with little air bubbles visible. This was no modern site, of this he was sure. Once the spring descended on the location with rains and warmer temperatures, the vegetation began to take over, along with the insects and snakes. His project was put on hold until next winter when the stone foundation would once again become visible.

When efforts were suspended, there were thirty-two stones revealed, several handmade bricks and a dozen hand-blown glass shards. The hut foundation was eighteen to twenty feet on one side and not yet halfway excavated. The original corner seems to be where a fireplace was located and where the broken glass pieces were found. Wood pieces uncovered from the soil are blackened as if they had been burned. There is still much work to do, but it seems there are exciting discoveries to be made.

The possibilities for this site are exciting to speculate about. The location tells a story because there were no plantation homes or roads in the area prior to the Civil War and all the way back to the colonial land records. There were two creeks, both about one hundred yards away. If this were a slave or indentured servant's quarters, it was not close to the owner's residence. The land it is located on and the adjacent land were undeveloped. That indicates that it was probably a runaway slave or indentured servant's hut because it would have been very difficult for someone to find it. It was then and is now way back in the woods.

That brings up the question about whether it could represent a hut or cabin of the vintage of Moll Dyer's era. Although it is probably too far from Moll Dyer Road, Moll Dyer Run and the site where the rock was found to be Moll's Hut site, it certainly might be a hut foundation from the same period. It might reveal some interesting secrets in the excavation process to shed light on the time when Moll Dyer roamed the woods in the area.

The resident wonders why he never took an interest until now to start to investigate these strange stones that have been hiding in plain sight all these years. Could Moll have whispered in his ear to look into what the possibilities

Pre–Civil War stone foundation excavation site of hut similar to that of Moll Dyer. *Photo by the author.*

are for this ancient foundation and to reveal the life of someone who might have shared some of her history? It will be interesting to unravel the story that these objects reveal in the months to come.

Another local Thompson is David W. Thompson, an author and descendant of the renowned Arthur Thompson. He is the author of a book titled *Sister Witch, The Life of Moll Dyer*, which is a fictionalized account of the life story of Moll Dyer that is completely fabricated except for the location where it unfolds as an enjoyable story.

David admits that he found very few facts in researching the woman Moll Dyer. He then decided to create her story in a book that would be the first of a series about the Dyer family in Southern Maryland. His story includes as many of the variations in the legend as he had heard. Some of those he heard from many sources as he grew up, including family and friends.

David found that the history of St. Mary's County during the colonial period provided interesting scenarios to entwine with the various stories that had come from different families who had been here for many generations. He didn't make any direct connection between those families and the demise of Moll Dyer and was not aware of the Thompson connection to the legend but admitted that association might have played a part in his interest in telling the story. He felt Moll was whispering in his ear to write her story, but maybe she was reaching out to a descendant of one of the original perpetrators. Could that be a common thread with the creation of this book?

David felt the guilt of being a citizen of the county where the residents had caused the death of this old woman blamed for circumstances beyond her control. He said, "As a St. Mary's Countian, I felt I owed Moll Dyer a personal debt, and justice was long overdue. My book was a labor of love and a posthumous apology of sorts. In it, Moll is cast as a tragic, yet heroic figure."

David shared a common guilty compassion for the tragedy of Moll Dyer. Was that the manifestation of the perceived curse so many years ago? He also agreed about the residents of this county and their hypocrisy toward Moll in respect to the founding of this colony on a basis of "religious tolerance." Not only were they intolerant with their pursuit of the "witch," but the basis for the entire witch persecution in this country was the result of the Puritans' relentless effort to impose their beliefs on the Catholics and Quakers. The key phrase here was "religious beliefs" were tolerated; witchcraft, when practiced with the help of Satan, was not considered a religious belief but rather an anti-religious belief and practice.

So, what about the legendary curse? Has it been perpetuated throughout the area and the generations who followed Moll Dyer? There definitely was the perception of one at the time, and it has been passed through generations ever since. The explanation for that is the mass guilt complex that endured with the people from the beginning. But, as the legend itself cannot be proved or disproved, neither can the presence of a curse. There certainly have been strange incidents that have happened to residents and the area in terms of weather and unexplained events in the area and surrounding the rock. Curses and spells are a two-way street. One has to make one, and the recipient has to acknowledge it. In this case, it is not known for sure that Moll made one, and it certainly doesn't seem that there are specific instances of dire consequences that anyone wants to believe are the result of any curse. In this case, whether Moll cursed those who persecuted her, those who did it believed that she must have cursed them and the entire area. Their belief in the curse gave it life and longevity. The possibility that there may be one will give this story legs for generations to come.

Epilogue

In looking back at this project, I think of it as a journey of discovery that took over my life in ways I could not have foreseen and revealed fascinating facts I could not have imagined. I think of the serendipitous beginning at the Mudd House and innocent curiosity of the connection between Sarah Frances Dyer Mudd and Moll Dyer. A sense of purpose began at the St. Mary's County Historical Society with a simple question and led me down many diverse paths since then. It has been difficult to comprehend all that has transpired, revealing an unbelievable circle of answers to many puzzles.

I am a mathematician, teacher and programmer by trade and a solver of puzzles innately. For twelve years, I raised and loved bloodhounds, known for their stubborn dedication to following a trail. I share this same characteristic combination of curiosity and tenacity. It made me the perfect candidate to unravel the mysterious trail of Moll Dyer. Moll tapped me on the shoulder and did not let go until the truth was told.

Early in the process, on August 16, 2013, I made a huge mistake and touched the Moll Dyer Rock in Leonardtown. The resulting episode of hemoptysis (bleeding from the lung) grabbed my attention and affirmed the possibility of a connection to this legend that made the research more than just an exercise in curiosity. As a result, I think it possible that Moll had a hand in that event in order to capture my attention and compel me to continue the effort to identify her. The rock remains in the center of Leonardtown today, and for me, it is still cursed.

To explain partially what happened when I touched the rock, I share a part of my personal medical history. I have a form of chronic obstructive pulmonary disease (COPD) called Bronchiectasis. As a result, I have a chronic condition called non-tubercular mycobacterium lung disease (NTM), one symptom of which is occasional slight bleeding from my lungs. About thirty seconds after touching the Moll Dyer Rock, my lungs began to bleed profusely (approximately one cup) for about forty-five minutes. The unusual volume and duration of this symptom upset and frightened my husband, Mike, and me. We were about to call 911 when it began to subside, and Mike remarked that it had begun right after I touched the rock.

Will I touch it again? Certainly not. Should you touch it? Go right ahead. Maybe my experience was totally coincidental with contacting it. I believe that some objects have a negative energy associated with them because something bad happened involving them. Did Moll die on that rock? It will never be known for sure, but it is entirely possible that she did. That part of the legend has survived for more than three hundred years. Believe what you will and touch it if you want to. Then see what happens.

This incident occurred after I had been researching the subject for several months. In thinking about it later, I began to believe that maybe Moll had reached out and tapped me on the shoulder to let me know that the curse was still working and to encourage me to pursue my efforts to identify her. Maybe there was something to the legend that Moll was a restless spirit in need of recognition, at least a real person who had existed and did not deserve her tragic end. There seemed to be a reason I was compelled to follow the trail of genealogical facts.

While I was compiling the facts and trees, trying to identify the woman who I believed to be Moll Dyer and composing a coherent paper to explain my findings, I was contacted by Susan Wolfe at the St. Mary's County Historical Society to ask permission to furnish my contact information to the Weather Channel. A producer there had approached her about a program that they wanted to shoot in Leonardtown about the Moll Dyer legend. They wanted to include the story for an episode in a series titled *Supernatural*. I told her that I would be happy to share my findings if they were interested.

I raced to finalize my article and copyright it because I knew that I would no longer have control over it once I gave them a digital copy. In January 2014, I was contacted by one of the producers and asked to participate in the filming of the program in the weeks following in Leonardtown. I discussed with her my research and the article that I had written. She asked that I forward a copy to her, which I subsequently did. I knew then that the research would be released for public scrutiny, and I would need to be prepared to defend the findings.

When the tornado made its appearance in Leonardtown during the filming, as covered in chapter 9, the path that it took was down Fairgrounds Road. That fact wouldn't mean anything to anyone else because I live on a small gravel road off Fairgrounds Road. When I heard that, I raced home to see what had happened. Driving down Fairgrounds Road to the road where I live, the chainsaws were buzzing as the county crew cut up several trees down along the road. When I turned down our road, all seemed fine until I drove up to the house. There in the front yard lay a grove of about twenty trees that had been leveled but, thankfully, not close enough to the house to have damaged it. My husband had just narrowly missed being in it as he arrived home from his daily bicycle ride and was still in the garage, which is detached from the house. He reported having heard the noise of a big wind right after he went inside. I thought about Moll and the Weather Channel and her doing some of her "weather magic" for their benefit.

After shooting the program, I shared my paper with Peter Himmelheber to be printed in the *Chronicles of St. Mary's*, the publication for the historical society. He worked on it with me and included it in the summer 2014 edition. I knew that I had to be prepared to defend my genealogical findings if they were questioned by anyone who read it. It was surprisingly quiet after the *Chronicles* came out, and I breathed a sigh of relief. I periodically checked the tree on Ancestry.com to make sure there were no "leafs" that popped up to give more information about my Mary Dyer. One did at one point, and I had a huge sinking feeling after publishing my findings. It indicated that Mary Dyer had a child and a husband. When I checked it out, it had been posted to the wrong sibling and was her sister's husband and child, thankfully.

The article, titled "In Search of Moll Dyer," was then published in the *Surratt Courier*, the monthly publication of the Surratt House Museum in Clinton, Maryland, and then later in the Samuel Mudd Society newsletter. Both times, I nervously awaited relatives of the Mudds and Dyers to receive the facts of my research, and I was not disappointed when the article came out in the Mudd newsletter. After success defending a couple of serious questions about the Dyer lineage, I felt confident that I could defend my research project as it continued to develop.

The year 2015 brought a new challenge for me as I applied for membership in the National Society of the Daughters of the American Revolution (NSDAR) and the local Major William Thomas chapter. With my interest in genealogy, I searched for my lineage on Ancestry.com. One thing that I found curious was that, although my colonial ancestors were all from North Carolina, I found that a brother to my seventeenth-century ancestor in North Carolina had traveled to St. Mary's County, Maryland, with another brother and a sister. I didn't think too much of it except for a curiosity about having a connection to where I now lived. When the chapter members learned of my Moll Dyer research, I was asked to give a program about it to the chapter. I did that with my charts of the lineages connected to Moll Dyer, including the DAR Patriot in the tree, and dressed in a period costume that I made. It was well received, and another career was launched.

In 2016 and 2017, I was asked to present my Moll Dyer program seven more times; each time, the program grew and eventually included a PowerPoint presentation, posters depicting the family trees and artifacts that would have been things that Moll might have had for her witchcraft practice. After the DAR presentation, I was asked to give talks at the College of Southern Maryland, the First Saints Community Church, Black Eyed Susan Doll Club, the Maryland Distillers Symposium, St. Mary's County Genealogy Society, the Surratt House Museum and the Front Porch Restaurant in the form of a walking tour to the rock. When I gave the presentation to the genealogy society, I felt that my research had withstood scrutiny at every level and survived unscathed. I was ready to write a book, which was a question I was asked at every event.

Actually, the program developed as I was reading every book I could find about seventeenth-century women to try to familiarize myself with the conditions that Moll faced, navigated and survived. I wasn't sure about the category of the book, whether to try historical fiction or keep it based on the facts that I could find. I decided that it would be based on the facts, since I had already written the foundation for it. In February 2016, I retreated to a home we owned in Tampa, Florida, for a month and immersed myself in the research and documentation from the resources to frame my life story for Moll Dyer. When I returned home, I began to create the narrative for the book.

When the narrative was done, I wanted to bring the story of Moll into the present and tie the legend to actual people who lived in that time as well as to the descendants of those people who still reside in St. Mary's County. The genealogical interest I had already pursued led me to the original land records of colonial Maryland and St. Mary's County. Many hours of examination revealed to me the residents of the county in 1697 and surprised me with my own relative in the midst of it. As I resolved and eliminated those who could not have been involved in Moll's fate, my own eleventh great-uncle Arthur Thompson was still standing all the way to the last Ten Most Likely. That has sparked a realization that maybe my five-year journey to uncover the mystery of Moll Dyer has been more than just a random event for my life story. In addition to the connection to Arthur Thompson, when I began the research into the empty tomb on Moll Dyer Road, it was a little unnerving to learn the name of the missing remains was Mary Bell Thompson, another strange coincidental fact with the Thompson name as well as the name Mary, again.

I have come to believe that maybe Moll's spirit and desire to be acknowledged have focused on me for some reason. The question about the connection between Sarah Frances Dyer Mudd and Moll Dyer drove me to do the research to resolve the question of Moll's very existence. From that research, I transitioned to the programs about Moll's genealogy and life story. From the enthusiastic reception of the subject and encouragement to put it in a book, this manuscript has finally come to fruition.

This book and the story of Moll's life were pieced together using the facts that came to light during lengthy research and weaving them into this historical narrative. The resulting story I believe fits the woman Mary Dyer, a simple player in a world that dictated her ultimate fate and death in St. Mary's County, Maryland. I have come to respect and celebrate her bravery and strength to have lived the life she did. I hope that the county and town of Leonardtown will share that appreciation for a woman who has brought so many interested and curious visitors to our area.

It is my opinion that the town of Leonardtown and St. Mary's County do owe an apology to Moll Dyer for burning down her hut and indirectly causing her to die a very horrible death that cold winter night. They did not know what is known today about witchcraft, weather and illnesses and acted to help themselves in the only way they thought they could. Another reason for them attributing a curse in her dying breath was probably because things didn't get better for them after she was dead. The only explanation they could come up with was that it had to have been a curse from her as she died. They felt that she was really angry at them and did swear at them for what they had done. That is entirely understandable and a self-fulfilling prophecy. Maybe it would bring some resolution and absolution to the residents and descendants of these people who brought this about to acknowledge this woman, who she really was and what really happened to her after all these years.

Being one of those who is related to one of the possible participants has been a total surprise. Did Moll choose me to tell her story because of my relationship to the people in this area? Did she know that I live close to her domain and wandered in "her" woods and wondered about her spirit being present? No matter the reason, it is hoped that justice has been done for her and as many facts as possible have been found to explain the entire story about a remarkable woman who suffered a terrible death as a result of the actions of her neighbors.

Maybe after the completion of this project, Moll will be done with me and let me move on knowing that I have done my best for her. My hope is that her spirit will finally rest in peace without malice directed toward this area or its residents, or at least the residents will no longer feel guilty.

Genealogical Research Details

As stated in chapter 4, the search began with the facts that were gleaned from all the articles that could be found about Moll Dyer and the people who claimed to be her relatives. The facts, as they were found, are as follows.

Journalist Philip Love wrote an article that states that "three Dyer men landed in St. Mary's County in 1690 after being chased out of England and Ireland because they were Catholics." Love goes on to claim that descendants of these three men included a Dr. Dyer, who practiced in Washington, D.C., and in Prince George's County, Maryland; Dr. Dyer's son, Father Edward Dyer, was the first American provincial of the Sulpician Order in the United States; and finally, these men were related to Moll Dyer, the St. Mary's County legendary witch, according to the article.[59] The object of the search was to find a Mary or Margaret Dyer the age of Moll with three brothers who immigrated to America and Maryland at the correct time. She had to have been a spinster and died around 1697.

The search began with the family tree for Sarah Frances Dyer and Reverend Edward Dyer to see where they led. See Tree Diagram Part 1 for the Sarah Frances Dyer Mudd family tree and lineage. This question originated out of curiosity as a result of the Dyer family connection to Dr. Samuel A. Mudd, with his wife being Sarah Frances Dyer Mudd. The answer regarding Sarah Frances Dyer's relationship to Moll Dyer is revealed by the fact that Sarah Frances Dyer Mudd is related to Moll Dyer (Mary Dyer, b. 1634) as a direct descendant of Moll's brother William Dyer (b. 1635).[60] Mary (Moll) Dyer is shown to be Sarah Frances Dyer's fourth great grand aunt.

Next, the tree for Edward Dyer was investigated. Reverend Edward Dyer was the first United States Provincial of Sulpician Order located in the United States.[61] See Tree Diagram Part 1 for Edward Dyer. He is also related to Moll Dyer (Mary Dyer, b. 1634) as a descendant of Moll's brother William Dyer (b. 1635). Mary (Moll) Dyer is Reverend Edward Dyer's fifth great grand aunt

Reverend Edward Dyer's father was Dr. John Ignatius Dyer, physician in Washington, D.C., and Prince George's County, Maryland.[62] He is also related to Moll Dyer (Mary Dyer, b. 1634) as a descendant of Moll's brother William Dyer (b. 1635). See Tree Diagram Part 1 for Edward Dyer. Mary (Moll) Dyer is Dr. John Ignatius Dyer's fourth great grand aunt.

In the follow-up article, "Search for Witch's Rock Leads to Tricky Knee," Philip Love goes on to quote from a letter from James Norman Simms of Silver Spring, Maryland. He claims that his mother, Mary Magdalene Dyer Simms, was a relative of Dr. Dyer, his son Reverend Edward Dyer and Moll Dyer, the witch.[63] In fact, Mary Magdalene Dyer Simms is shown to be related to Moll Dyer (Mary Dyer, b. 1634) as a descendant of Moll's brother William Dyer (b. 1635).[64] See Tree Diagram Part 1 for Mary Dyer Simms. Mary (Moll) Dyer is Mary Magdalene Dyer Simms's fourth great grand aunt.

In the article "Myth Is as Good as a Mile in Hunt for Witch's Rock," Philip H. Love claims that Marie "Mattie" Dyer Purcell's father was a relative of Moll Dyer.[65] Marie "Mattie" Dyer Purcell is related to Moll Dyer (Mary Dyer, b. 1634) as a descendant of Moll's brother William Dyer (b. 1635).[66] See Tree Diagram Part 2 for Mattie Dyer Purcell to see this lineage. Mary (Moll) Dyer is Marie "Mattie" Dyer Purcell's sixth great grand aunt.

The final claim regarding Moll Dyer is that a gentleman named William Kane and his mother, Deborah Ann Dyer Kane, are related to Moll Dyer. This is the premise of an article titled "Finding a Witch in the Family Tree," written by Susan Craton.[67] In fact, William Kane and his mother, Deborah Ann Dyer, are related to Moll Dyer. This claim is true, and the relationship is through Moll Dyer's (Mary Dyer, b. 1634) father's cousin.[68] See Tree Diagram Part 2 for William Kane and his lineage. Thomas Dyer (b. 1590) is Mary (Moll) Dyer's great uncle; he is also William Kane's tenth great-grandfather. They are related to Moll as distant cousins.

After developing these trees and finding the same woman named Mary Dyer present in all of them, the identity of the elusive Moll Dyer was revealed as the logical conclusion. The William Dyer descendants who met all these requirements at the beginning of the seventeenth century were identified.

Mary Dyer was born on February 19, 1634, in Kenn, Devon (Devonshire), England, to William Dyer (born December 31, 1607) and Elizabeth Holcombe, who were married in 1629.[69] She had a brother William, born in 1635, and a brother Thomas, born in 1625.[70]

From the identity of Mary Dyer, research revealed the following sequence of events. The examination of immigration records disclosed her journey from England to Maryland.

The facts concerning their immigration to America from England are as follows:

On October 25, 1669, Mary Dyer of Bristol, England, was apprenticed to Thomas Lugg for four years at Nevis Plantation, St. Kitts, West Indies, to pay off her passage.[71]

On October 29, 1669, Edward Dyer of Bristol, England, was apprenticed to John Bullock for four years in Barbados on Leewards to pay for his passage.[72]

On December 3, 1669, William Dyer of Bristol, England, was apprenticed to George Salter for four years at Nevis Plantation, St. Kitts, West Indies, to pay for his passage.[73]

On November 8, 1677, Mary Dyer immigrated to Dorchester County, Maryland, and was transported there by Captain Thomas Taylor.[74] From there, it is assumed that she traveled to St. Mary's County and took up residence south of where the city of Leonardtown is today as an indentured servant on land that was part of an area known as St. Margaret's or Lewgers Plains.[75] There are no records of her marriage, children, death or burial in the area.

William, Edward and Mary Dyer left England in 1669, and Mary arrived in Maryland in 1677 after an eight-year indenture at Nevis Plantation, St. Kitts.[76] Brother Thomas came in 1671.[77] William Dyer arrived in Virginia in 1674.[78]

The legendary claim that three Dyer men landed in Maryland in 1690 after being chased out of England and Ireland is close to reality. In fact, there were three Dyer men who immigrated to America and a Mary Dyer who arrived in Maryland from England at various times, but none in 1690.[79]

All these facts, taken together, identify Mary Dyer, born in 1634 in Devon, England, to William Dyer and Elizabeth Holcombe, as the legendary witch of St. Mary's County, Moll Dyer. After the record of her birth (baptism) and the records of her immigration to Maryland in 1677 with her brothers William and Thomas (and relative Edward) via the Nevis Plantation indenture in 1669, there is no record of her marriage or death, making

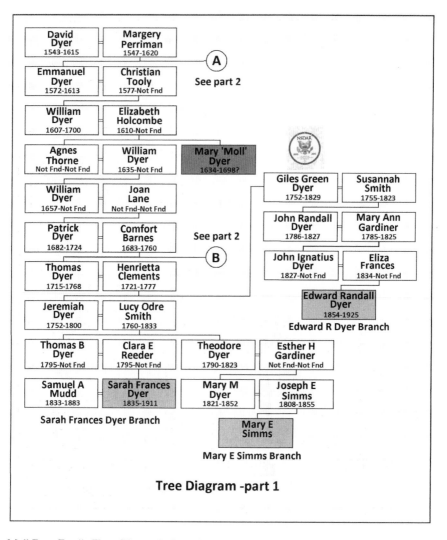

Tree Diagram -part 1

Moll Dyer Family Tree. *Diagram by Peter Himmelheber, St. Mary's County Historical Society.*

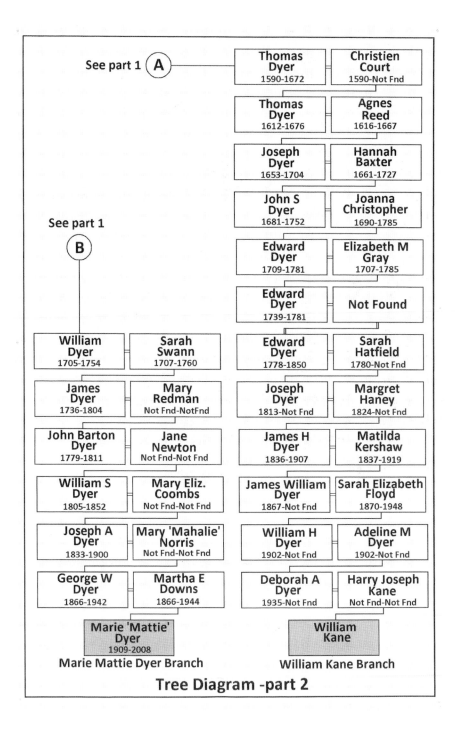

See part 1 (A) — Thomas Dyer 1590-1672 = Christien Court 1590-Not Fnd

Thomas Dyer 1612-1676 = Agnes Reed 1616-1667

Joseph Dyer 1653-1704 = Hannah Baxter 1661-1727

John S Dyer 1681-1752 = Joanna Christopher 1690-1785

Edward Dyer 1709-1781 = Elizabeth M Gray 1707-1785

Edward Dyer 1739-1781 = Not Found

See part 1 (B)

William Dyer 1705-1754 = Sarah Swann 1707-1760

Edward Dyer 1778-1850 = Sarah Hatfield 1780-Not Fnd

James Dyer 1736-1804 = Mary Redman Not Fnd-NotFnd

Joseph Dyer 1813-Not Fnd = Margret Haney 1824-Not Fnd

John Barton Dyer 1779-1811 = Jane Newton Not Fnd-Not Fnd

James H Dyer 1836-1907 = Matilda Kershaw 1837-1919

William S Dyer 1805-1852 = Mary Eliz. Coombs Not Fnd-Not Fnd

James William Dyer 1867-Not Fnd = Sarah Elizabeth Floyd 1870-1948

Joseph A Dyer 1833-1900 = Mary 'Mahalie' Norris Not Fnd-Not Fnd

William H Dyer 1902-Not Fnd = Adeline M Dyer 1902-Not Fnd

George W Dyer 1866-1942 = Martha E Downs 1866-1944

Deborah A Dyer 1935-Not Fnd = Harry Joseph Kane Not Fnd-Not Fnd

Marie 'Mattie' Dyer 1909-2008

Marie Mattie Dyer Branch

William Kane

William Kane Branch

Tree Diagram -part 2

her an elderly spinster in St. Mary's County in 1697. She learned about "witchcraft" (herbal remedies, spells and voodoo) while at Nevis Plantation and brought that knowledge with her. She continued as an indigent resident on the land known as St. Margaret's in St. Mary's County until her death in 1697.

Notes

Chapter 1

1. Beitzell, "Legends of St. Mary's Moll Dyer."
2. Babcock, "Witch or Not."

Chapter 2

3. The information presented in this chapter is from Cooke, *Witch Trials, Legends, & Lore of Maryland*, 30–53, and Parke, "Witchcraft in Maryland," 271–76, 281–98. The facts will be paraphrased instead of using direct quotations to make this text more relevant for readers to understand the details of the historical events surrounding the tragic death of Moll Dyer.
4. Glanvill, *Saducismus Triumphatus*.
5. Rebecca Morehouse, MAC Lab State Curator, August 2009.

Chapter 3

6. Maryland State Archives, Dr. Lois Green Carr's Biographical Files of 17th and 18th Century Marylanders, Men's Career Files, MSA SC 5094, image number sc5094-0352-01.

7. Ibid., image number sc5094-0352-05.

8. Ibid., image number sc5094-0404-0121-3.

9. Ibid., image number sc5094-0352-14.

10. Ibid., image number sc5094-4071-8.

11. Ibid., image number sc5094-4071-9.

Chapter 5

12. SFDyer Family Tree, ancestry.com; England, Select Births and Christenings, 1538–1975, FHL Film Number 916850.

13. Barbados Act for the Better Ordering and Governing of Negroes, 23940.

14. Olmert, "Treating the Enslaved," 98.

Chapter 6

15. *Settlers of Maryland, 1679–1783*, Maryland State Archives (online), ancestry.com.

16. Menard, "Tract Map."

17. St. Mary's County Tax Records for New Town Hundred, 1707.

18. Maryland State Archives, Dr. Lois Green Carr's Biographical Files of 17th and 18th Century Marylanders, Men's Career Files, MSA SC 5094, image number sc5094-4070-15.

19. Love, "Witch to Remember."

20. 1930 U.S. Census, Leonardtown, St. Mary's, Maryland, Roll 879, Page 44, Enumeration District 0006, FHL microfilm 2340614.

21. U.S. WWII Draft Cards Young Men, 1940–1947 (online), Ancestry.com.

22. 1940 U.S. Census, St. Mary's, Maryland, Roll T627_1559, Page 8B, Enumeration District 19-12.

23. Reports of Deaths of American Citizens Abroad, 1835–1974 (database online), Provo, UT, USA, Ancestry.com, 2010.

24. U.S. Social Security Death Index, 1935–2014 (database online), Provo, UT, USA, Ancestry.com, 2011.

25. Ibid.

26. MSA, Image No. sc5094-0822-1.

27. *Maryland, Calendar of Wills*, 1635–1743 (online database), Provo, UT, Ancestry.com, 1998.

28. Maryland State Archives, Dr. Lois Green Carr's Biographical Files of 17th and 18th Century Marylanders, Men's Career Files, MSA SC 5094, image number sc5094-1589-1.

29. Ibid., image number sc5094-2244-02.

30. Maguire, *Jarboe Family Book*, will dated January 1708.

31. Maryland State Archives, Dr. Lois Green Carr's Biographical Files of 17th and 18th Century Marylanders, Men's Career Files, MSA SC 5094, image number sc5094-3066-04.

32. Ibid., image numbers sc5094-1417-01,02,05,06,07.

33. Ibid., image numbers sc5094-4162-01,02,03,05,06,22,28.

34. Ibid., image number sc5094-4521-01.

35. Cameron et al., *America's First*, 32–33.

36. Maryland State Archives, Dr. Lois Green Carr's Biographical Files of 17th and 18th Century Marylanders, Men's Career Files, MSA SC 5094, image number sc5094-1234-1.

37. Jane Baldwin Cotton, *Maryland, Calendar of Wills*, vol. 6, book 19, page 433, Ancestry.com.

Chapter 7

38. U.S. Census, 1940, index and images, John Thomas Hatfield, Election District 3, St. Mary's, Maryland, United States; citing enumeration district (ED) 19-7, sheet 12A, family 175, NARA digital publication of T627, roll 1559, familysearch.org.

39. http://www.singletonfamily.org, accessed December 8, 2014.

40. U.S. Social Security Death Index, Social Security Administration, Social Security Death Index, Master File, ancestry.com.

41. U.S. Census, 1900, index and images, Mary B. Thompson in household of Rolt Thompson, Statesburg Township, Sumter, South Carolina, United States; citing sheet 5A, family 88, NARA microfilm publication T623, FHL microfilm 1241543, familysearch.org, accessed September 24, 2014.

42. U.S. Census, 1910, Sumter Ward 2, Sumter, South Carolina Roll T624_1465, page 26A, Enumeration District 0122, FHL microfilm 1375478, ancestry.com, accessed December 15, 2014.

43. U.S. Census, 1910, index and images, Mary B. Thompson in household of Robert Thompson, Statesburg, Sumter, South Carolina, United States; citing enumeration district (ED) 117, sheet 10A, family 151, NARA

microfilm publication T624, FHL microfilm 1375478, familysearch.org, accessed September 24, 2014,

44. U.S. Census, 1920, Sumter Ward 1, Sumter, South Carolina, Roll T625_1713, Page 6A, Enumeration District 149, image 214, ancestry.com, accessed December 15,2014.

45. U.S. Census, 1920, index and images, Joseph Brown, Saint George, Dorchester, South Carolina, United States, citing sheet 9A, family 220, NARA microfilm publication T625, FHL microfilm 1821693, familysearch.org, accessed October 8, 2014.

46. U.S. Census, 1930, Statesburg, Sumter, South Carolina, Roll 2214, Page 5B, Enumeration District 0024, Image 116.0, FHL microfilm 2341948, ancestry.com, accessed December 15, 2014.

47. U.S. Census, 1930, McLauchlin, Hoke, North Carolina, Roll 1699, Page 4B, Enumeration District 0008, image 799.0, FHL microfilm 2341433, ancestry.com, accessed June 18, 2014.

48. "North Carolina, Deaths, 1931–1994," index, Sam Jacobs, 12 Apr 1931, citing, Hoke, North Carolina, can 43, State Department of Archives and History, Raleigh, FHL microfilm 1943036, familysearch.org, accessed October 8, 2014.

49. U.S. Census, 1940, Sumter, Sumter, South Carolina, Roll T627_3842, Page 8A, Enumeration District 434, familysearch.org, accessed December 15, 2014.

50. U.S. Census, 1940, index and images, John Thomas Hatfield, Election District 3, St. Mary's, Maryland, United States; citing enumeration district (ED) 19-7, sheet 12A, family 175, NARA digital publication of T627, roll 1559, familysearch.org, accessed November 8, 2013.

51. The National Archives at St. Louis, St. Louis, Missouri, World War II Draft Cards (Fourth Registration) for the State of Maryland, State Headquarters, Maryland, Microfilm Series M1939, Microfilm Roll 25, ancestry.com, accessed December 17, 2014.

52. Clerk of the Circuit Court (Land Records), St. Mary's County Court House, Leonardtown, MD [hereafter LR] Book JMM 11, page 123. These records are online at mdlandrec.net/main, accessed January 17, 2016.

53. Ibid., 172.

54. Death Certificate, St. Mary's County, Maryland, Mary Bell Thompson Jacobs, July 12, 1942; copy from Maryland Archives, 12 December 2014.

55. U.S. Census, 1910, index and images, Washington Jacobs Jr. in household of Washington Jacobs, Statesburg, Sumter, South Carolina, United States; citing enumeration district (ED) 117, sheet 18B, family

274, NARA microfilm publication T624, National Archives and Records Administration, Washington, D.C.; FHL microfilm 1,375,478, familysearch.org, December 13, 2014.

56. LR, Book CBB 13, page 518.

57. U.S. Social Security Death Index, Social Security Administration, Social Security Death Index, Master File, ancestry.com.

58. "3 Charged in Bizarre Grave Case," *Enterprise* (Leonardtown, MD), January 28, 1965.

Appendix

59. Love, "Myth Is as Good," "Search for Witch's Rock," 380–81.

60. Mudd, *Mudd Family*, 524; SFDyer Family Tree.

61. St. Mary's Seminary and University Associated Archives, Associated Sulpicians of the United States Archives, www.stmarys.edu.

62. Craton, "Finding a Witch."

63. Love, "Myth Is as Good," "Search for Witch's Rock."

64. SFDyer Family Tree.

65. Love, "Myth Is as Good," "Search for Witch's Rock."

66. SFDyer Family Tree.

67. 1658–1758 Charles County, Maryland, Families, "The First 100 Years," ancestry.com, accessed June 9, 2013.

68. Clayton Howard Family Tree, Geary Family Tree, William Dyer (1607–1700), ancestry.com.

69. England Births and Christenings, 1538–1975 index, familysearch.org.

70. Clayton Howard Family Tree, Geary Family Tree, William Dyer (1607–1700).

71. Coldham, *Complete Book of Emigrants*, 259.

72. Ibid., 260.

73. Ibid., 261.

74. U.S. and Canada Passenger and Immigration lists.

75. Menard, "Tract Map."

76. Skordas, *Early Settlers of Maryland*, 143.

77. Coldham, *Complete Book of Emigrants*, 261.

78. Nugent, *Cavaliers and Pioneers*, 156.

79. 1658–1758 Charles County, Maryland, Families.

References

Babcock, Jason. "Witch or Not, Moll Dyer Legend Lives On." *Southern Maryland Enterprise*, October 30, 2009.

Barbados Act for the Better Ordering and Governing of Negroes, September 27, 1661, Barbados MSS Laws, 1645–1682, c.o. 30/2/16-26.

Barratt, John. *The Civil War in the West*. Bamsley, South Yorkshire, UK: Pen & Sword Military, 2005.

Beitzell, Edwin, ed. "Legends of St. Mary's Moll Dyer." *Chronicles of St. Mary's* 16, no. 12 (December 1968).

Browne, William Hand. *Proceedings and Acts of the General Assembly of Maryland April 1666–June 1676*. Baltimore: Maryland Historical Society, 1884.

Cameron, Timothy K., Grace Mary Brady, Jeffrey McLane, Carol Moody, Linda Reno and Mary Ann Thompson. *America's First, A History of America's Oldest Continuously Operating Sheriff's Office*. 2nd ed. Gwynn Oak, MD: United Book Press, 2017.

Coldham, Peter Wilson. *The Complete Book of Emigrants 1661–1699*. Baltimore, MD: Genealogical Publishing Company, 1990.

Cooke, William H. *Witch Trials, Legends, & Lore of Maryland: Dark, Strange and True Tales*. Annapolis, MD: Undertaker Press, 2012.

Craton, Susan. "Finding a Witch in the Family Tree." *Southern Maryland Enterprise*, April 1, 2005.

Dunn, Richard S. *Sugar & Slaves: The Rise of the Planter Class in the English West Indies, 1624–1713*. Chapel Hill: University of North Carolina Press, 1972.

1880 United States Census. Familysearch.org.

Emerson, Kathy Lynn. *The Writer's Guide to Everyday Life in Renaissance England from 1485–1649*. Cincinnati, OH: Writer's Digest Books, 1996.

Evening Star. "A Witch to Remember." November 20, 1972.

Few, Janet. *Coffers, Clysters, Comfrey and Coifs: The Lives of Our Seventeenth Century Ancestors*. Lancashire, UK: Family History Partnership, 2012.

Filby, P. William, ed. *Passenger and Immigration Lists Index 1500s–1900s*. Farmington Hills, MI: Gale Research, 2010.

Fraser, Antonia. *The Weaker Vessel*. New York: Alfred A. Knopf, 1984.

Glanvill, Joseph, *Saducismus Triumphatus, or Full and Plain Evidence Concerning Witches and Apparitions: In Two Parts; The First Treating of Their Possibility, the Second of Their Real Existence*. London, 1681.

Gordon, Joyce. *Nevis, Queen of the Caribees*. London: MacMillan Caribbean, 1985.

Handlin, Oscar, and Mary F. Handlin. "Origins of the Southern Labor System." *William and Mary Quarterly* 7, 3rd series (1950): 221.

Higham, C.S. *The Development of the Leeward Islands Under the Restoration, 1660–1688*. Cambridge, UK: University Press, 1921.

Hubbard, Vincent K. *Swords, Ships & Sugar: History of Nevis*. Corvallis, OR: Premiere Editions International, 2002.

Iles, John Alexander Burke. *An Account Descriptive of the Island of Nevis*. N.p.: British Library, Historic, 2011.

Logan, Rebecca L. "Witches and Poisoners in the Colonial Chesapeake." PhD diss., Union Institute, 2001.

Love, Philip H., ed. "Myth Is as Good as a Mile In Hunt for Witch's Rock"; "Search for Witch's Rock Leads to Tricky Knee," "Witch to Remember." Washington Star and North American Newspaper Alliance, reprinted in *Chronicles of St. Mary's*, vol. 5, *1967–1970*. 379–81. N.p., n.d.

Maguire, Mary Jo. *The Jarboe Family Book*. Self-published, 1977.

Maryland Calendar of Wills. Baltimore, MD: Kohn & Pollock Inc., 1904–1928. Ancestry.com.

Menard, Russell R. "A Tract Map for St. Mary's County in 1705." *Chronicles of St. Mary's* 21 (May 1973).

Mortimer, Ian. *The Time Traveler's Guide to Elizabethan England*. New York: Penguin Books, 2012.

Mudd, Dr. Richard D. *The Mudd Family of the United States*. Saginaw, MI: self-published, 1951.

Nevis Act of May 26, 1675. *Leeward Island Laws, 1668–1682*, c.o. 154/2/107-108.

Nugent, Nell Marion. *Cavaliers and Pioneers: Abstracts of Virginia Land Patents and Grants*. Vol. 2, *1666–1695*. Richmond: Virginia State Library, 1977.

Olmert, Michael. "Treating the Enslaved: The Method of Medical Care Varied from Plantation to Plantation." *Trend and Tradition: The Magazine of Colonial Williamsburg* (Spring 2017): 98.

Parke, Francis Neal. "Witchcraft in Maryland." *Maryland Historical Magazine* 31, no. 4 (December 1936): 287–89.

Picard, Liza. *Restoration London, Everyday Life in London 1660–1670*. London: Phoenix Paperback, 1997.

Provincial Court to the Maryland State Archives, 1683–1706, S547, Transcribed by Francis Neal Parke.

Quaife, G.R. *Wanton Wenches and Wayward Wives: Peasants and Illicit Sex in Early Seventeenth-Century England*. Abingdon, UK: Routledge, 1979.

Skordas, Gust, ed. *The Early Settlers of Maryland*. Baltimore, MD: Genealogical Publishing, 1968.

Thompson, Janet A. *Wives, Widows, Witches, and Bitches: Women in Seventeenth-Century Devon*. New York: Peter Lang, 1993.

Turner, Louise. *Life in Maryland in the Seventeenth Century*. N.p.: National Society of the Colonial Dames of America in the State of Maryland, 2003.

Williams, Eric Eustace. *From Columbus to Castro: The History of the Caribbean, 1492–1969*. London: A. Deutsch, 2003.

Wright, Louis B. *The Cultural Life of the American Colonies, 1607–1763*. New York: Harper and Row Publishers, 1957.

Index

About the Author

Lynn Buonviri has been a resident of St. Mary's County, Maryland, since 1981, and like her husband, Mike, is retired from St. Mary's County Public Schools (SMCPS). She was a teacher and Information Technology (IT) professional throughout the forty years of her career. She started as a programmer for the Apollo Program at the National Aeronautics and Space Administration (NASA) in 1967 and ended as a system administrator for the school system. In the midst of her IT career, she taught mathematics at A.C. Jones High School in Beeville, Texas, before coming to St. Mary's County, where she taught at St. Mary's Ryken and Great Mills High Schools, Margaret Brent Middle School and Charles County Community College. Lynn has a bachelor of science degree in mathematics from Auburn University and a master of science in information systems from University of Maryland University College.

Her interests since retirement are writing, genealogy and doll collecting, restoration, preservation and education, with a focus on the colonial period and the Civil War. She shares her collection of dolls of the Civil War period with displays at the Mudd House Annual Victorian Christmas and annual Christmas display at the St. Clements Island Patuxent River Museum.

She currently volunteers as a docent at the Surratt House and Tavern Museum in Clinton, Maryland, and the Dr. Samuel A. Mudd House Museum in Waldorf, Maryland. It was in this capacity that her interest in the Moll Dyer story began.

Lynn travels to area organizations to present her programs on the history of Civil War dolls, Moll Dyer, Mary Surratt, Dr. Samuel A. Mudd and Private Jane Perkins of the Danville Light Artillery Unit of the Army of Northern Virginia. She is a lifelong seamstress and always dresses in period costumes she makes herself.

She is also the registrar for the Major William Thomas chapter of the NSDAR and assists prospective members with the application process. It is in this capacity that her interest in genealogy is constantly put to the test.

She is the author of *Mary's Story*, a historical fiction book about Mary Surratt, and has written several short stories featuring doll adventures, usually in conjunction with events sponsored by the Black Eyed Susan Doll Club. This is Lynn's second book to be published.